D0983645

NASHVILLE

CITYSCOPES: a unique overview of a city's past as well as a focused eye on its present. Written by authors with intimate knowledge of the cities, each book provides a historical account with essays on the city today. Together these offer fascinating vignettes on the quintessential and the quirky, the old and the new. Illustrated throughout with compelling historical images as well as contemporary photos, these are essential cultural companions to the world's greatest cities.

Titles in the series:

CITYSCOPES

Nashville

Music and Manners

Richard Schweid

REAKTION BOOKS

For Emanuele Nastasi, who is a Nashvillian at heart;
For Anne Paine, who is Nashville at its best

Published by Reaktion Books Ltd
Unit 32, Waterside
44–48 Wharf Road
London N1 7UX, UK

www.reaktionbooks.co.uk

First published 2021
Copyright © Richard Schweid 2021

Printed and bound in India by Replika Press Pvt. Ltd

A catalogue record for this book is available from the British Library
ISBN 978 1 78914 315 7

OPENING IMAGES p. 6 (top): Tennessee State Capitol building; p. 6 (bottom): front view
of Ryman Auditorium; p. 7: lobby of the Union Station hotel; p. 8: people on the Broadway
strip; p. 9 (top): bowling alley at Pinewood Social; p. 9 (bottom): the Gateway Boulevard
Bridge; p. 10 (top): fireworks over Nashville's New Year's Eve celebrations; p. 10 (bottom):
Downtown Nashville skyline at sunset, the week before the NFL draft; p. 11 (top): the
Parthenon in Centennial Park; p. 11 (bottom): inside the Country Music Hall of Fame
and Museum; p. 12: Printer's Alley; p. 13 (top): staircase in the Union Station hotel;
p. 13 (bottom): neon sign for a downtown clothing store and gift shop; p. 14: sign
outside the Johnny Cash Museum; p. 15: guitar sign in front of the Legends Corner
bar. HISTORY p. 29: the yard of a military hospital, 1863. THE CITY TODAY p. 133:
Downtown Nashville. LISTINGS p. 191: an evening of country music at Tootsies
Orchid Lounge.

Contents

Belle Meade Mansion, built in 1853.

Prologue: A City in Transition

I was born in 1946, into a post-Second World War Nashville, a city that was God-fearing and Bible-reading, where alcohol was not served in restaurants, and the races were strictly—but not equally—divided, with white people getting most of the spoils. In that year, Nashville was a city that prided itself on being an intellectual center of the Southeastern United States, home to some of the South's finest universities, yet only 22 years earlier, it was still illegal to teach Darwin's theory of evolution in Tennessee's public schools. Biology teachers were required to explain the birth of the world, and its inhabitants, using the creation myth described in Genesis: six long workdays for the Lord.

The Nashville of my birth was a prosperous, second-tier southern city, where old money called the shots: bankers, insurers, realtors who all belonged to the same churches, the same exclusive country clubs, and sent their children to the same private schools. These members of what was referred to as "old Nashville" came from white, moneyed, Protestant families of long-standing in the community, and they pulled the strings of whatever puppet politicians were in office, shaping Nashville's municipal policies to their liking.

These old-money Nashvillians looked down with faint scorn on the newly wealthy, who had accumulated their riches in one generation by working in the up-and-coming country music industry. These record company executives and star performers were considered arrivistes, the nouveau riche, uncouth, unmannered boors who drove flashy new cars and were relegated to garish, newly constructed mansions on the edge of the city, rather than the imposing, brick-and-stone estates of the exclusive Belle Meade neighborhood, which dated back to the early 1800s.

This Gentile, genteel, all-American Nashville of my childhood—surrounded by woods, fertile farmlands, rolling hills, and rivers—was said to have more churches per capita than any other city in the nation, and was often referred to as "the buckle on the Bible belt." Church still comes first for many Nashvillians, and it is not unusual to hear people in a public place—standing in line at a supermarket check-out counter, for instance—having a hermeneutic discussion about the finer points of a given biblical verse. David Halberstam, in his wonderful book about the city's civil rights movement, *The Children*, wrote of the 1950s, "Nashville was a great center for colleges and religious education. The Protestant Vatican some people called it, because it was the headquarters for so many Southern religious groups, their publishing arms, and their sectarian colleges."

While it is still proudly Protestant, the years since then have wrought a sea change in the city, although exactly when that transformation began depends on whom you ask. A political scientist might say the modern life of Nashville began in 1963, when voters agreed to merge the city and surrounding Davidson County, creating one metropolitan government where there had been two. Other people will point to 1967, when it finally became legal to buy a mixed drink in a restaurant or a bar, or to 1975, with the release of Robert Altman's film *Nashville*, as the moment at which the nation's collective cultural consciousness first took note of the city's existence. Still others might delay the date until October 2012, when the ABC television network debuted *Nashville,* which proved to be a long-running prime-time weekly series, or January 2013, when a *New York Times* article deemed Nashville an "It" city. Regardless of when the city began its metamorphosis, by 2017 it was no longer a second-tier, old-guard city, but instead an iconic destination both for young people looking to move their lives to new surroundings, and those country music fans just looking to spend a little time in their Mecca. For all its problems, Nashville was an exciting place to live or visit.

For Southerners, Nashville has long represented intellect, culture, and downright fun, known as a city both refined and raucous,

Schermerhorn Symphony Center.

capable of embracing antebellum mansions and manners, as well as honky-tonks, trailer parks, dirt farmers, and down-home living. It is a place that houses the Frist Museum of Contemporary Art cheek-by-jowl with the Country Music Hall of Fame and Museum. Music lovers will turn out to fill the beautiful New Classical architecture of the Schermerhorn Symphony Center for a Nashville Symphony Orchestra concert, and they will also pack the Ryman Auditorium for an evening listening to Ricky Skaggs.

The city has a particular culinary tradition, all its own. Lately, its cuisine has been hailed nationwide for its "hot chicken," a fried chicken coated with hellish heat, but long before the recent burst of publicity, when New York foodies and travel writers discovered this longtime local favorite, the best of Nashville's home cooking was available at numerous "meat-and-three" restaurants. These places served, and continue to serve, a reasonably priced lunch of just that: a meat with three side dishes, chosen from a long steam table holding an appetizing range of possibilities, mostly "soul food" out of the toothsome African American kitchen—things like turnip greens, collard greens, baked squash casserole, fried okra, black-eyed peas, yams, or fried green tomatoes, always with cornbread to sop up the

Country Music Hall of Fame.

juices. Europe contributed to the meat side of the steam table when English and Irish settlers in the eighteenth and nineteenth centuries brought pigs and chickens, a bounty perhaps best appreciated at the city's notable array of restaurants serving top-notch barbecue.

Food in Nashville has been a bond between the city's various races and ethnicities, a cuisine drawn from its different residents. Over the past couple of decades, what people eat, like the racial and ethnic mix of the city itself, has gone from being basically white or black, to having lots of colors in between. African American and European American dishes are now supplemented by a wide variety of excellent ethnic cuisines, ranging from Vietnamese, African, and Latin American, to Middle Eastern.

In many other ways, as well, the city was transformed over the first two decades of the twenty-first century. Nashville regularly appears in surveys alongside cities such as Los Angeles and New York as a place where people would most like to live. Every day in 2017, according to the local Chamber of Commerce, more than one hundred newcomers arrived with their hopes and dreams. Many of them came from places such as Los Angeles or Manhattan. Most of them were young and white, looking for a prosperous, green city in which to raise their families, somewhere far from the mad urban rush they had known on the coasts. Ironically, to accommodate all this new blood, Nashville has shucked its modest pace of life, and transformed itself into a booming metropolis, with lots of traffic clogging inadequate roads, chock-a-block with office towers and hotels; it is one of the fastest growing cities in the u.s., with a skyrocketing housing market, in which the prices of both home ownership and rental have drastically increased. The poor and middle class are increasingly priced out of neighborhoods. A number of industries play important roles in the city's economy, including health care, banking, religious publishing, private prisons, and insurance, all in addition to the music industry. Tourism increases annually, and visitors flock to sites like the Country Music Hall of Fame and Museum. Tourism revenue in 2017 was about $6.5 billion, much of it thanks to the draw of the music industry, but more and more businesses are relocating as well. Tennessee is a right-to-work state, where it is difficult for unions to organize workplaces like construction sites and factories, and it's a good state in which to produce cheaply. In May 2018, British Airways initiated a nonstop London-to-Nashville flight to serve both business and tourism interests, and in November of that year, Amazon announced that it would build an East Coast "operations center" in Nashville, creating some 5,000 new jobs.

When I was growing up, the part of town referred to as Lower Broad, the first six long blocks stretching up Broadway from the Cumberland River, was tenanted with shabby honky-tonk beer bars, stores that sold western clothing, and a couple of record shops, all anchored by the Ryman Auditorium, known as the Mother Church of country music. The Ryman was originally built as a gospel tabernacle in 1898 to preach and sing the Word, and, subsequently, it was the home of a weekly live radio broadcast begun in 1925 on the radio station wsm, a Saturday-night program of country music. Initially, the show went out as the wsm Barn Dance, and was rechristened two years later as the Grand Ole Opry. WSM had a mighty signal, and people tuned in across much of the country.

As recently as 1990, a person could just about have put a chair out on the corner of Fourth Avenue South and Broadway—close by the Ryman—during any long afternoon, and sat for a considerable spell without more than a couple of dozen people passing by. Most Nashvillians did not so much consciously avoid going to Lower Broad; they simply never had a reason to do so. The shadowy honky-tonks didn't serve anything more alcoholic than a cold can of Pabst Blue Ribbon beer, and the folks that sat at the bars to drink it in the afternoons were mostly poor, white men, some of whom were a good bet to finish the day in jail.

Still, aspiring country musicians were welcome to play at places like Tootsie's Orchid Lounge, which was right around the corner

Ryman Auditorium interior, 2012.

Tootsie's Orchid Lounge, a Lower Broad icon.

from the Ryman, and where someone playing for tips might be heard by someone in the music industry who had come in for a cold one. The whole area, encompassing the Ryman, the Ernest Tubb Record Shop, and the honky-tonks, had a certain derelict authenticity. As a young man, photographer Bill Rouda spent a lot of time hanging around, absorbing that feeling and reflecting it in his photographs. His shots of those years were gathered in a book, *Nashville's Lower Broad: The Street That Music Made*. He acknowledged that his work documents a time that is gone and will not come again. "Tourism has changed life on Lower Broad for sure," he wrote me in an email from his current home in North Carolina.

> I don't know where all the homeless have gone but I suspect they're still homeless. I was always taken by the caring and generosity a few local bar owners (and others like musicians or singer-songwriters) offered the homeless. Robert Moore of

Robert's Western World and Mama Joe Eaton, owner of The Music City Lounge, always had a Thanksgiving meal for the disenfranchised and anybody and everybody else that needed it.

The music did seem to help keep things tranquil much of the time, but other times it was hard to tell what might happen next. Alcoholism was in the mix too. Old Lower Broad may have looked to be at the bottom of a swamp somewhere but many I met there truly were fine people, maybe finer than any country club or many churches I've been in.

These days and nights, the sidewalks of Lower Broad are inhabited by out-of-town visitors, a constant flood tide of people willing to pay high prices for a cocktail, a glass of expensive wine, or a craft beer at one of numerous brightly lit establishments, neon signs marking them, country music booming out of all their doorways. These tourists are paying for high-priced hotel rooms, and eating in nice restaurants, where any kind of liquor they want is available. Every few minutes, a "pedal tavern" carrying a dozen young bachelorettes from other places, who are here celebrating a friend's impending wedding, rolls by in the middle of the street, the celebrants swilling beer, peddling, and whooping it up in plain sight, right in front of God and everybody. Parking places are at a premium, even at $20 an hour. In 2018 a study by the Department of Public Works found that foot traffic on Lower Broad was as dense as Times Square in New York City.

Current rents on Lower Broad are far too expensive for real honky-tonks, which are likely to have much smaller income streams than today's tourist venues. By definition, a Nashville honky-tonk is not really a place where most tourists are likely to feel comfortable—particularly with Tennessee's gun laws, which permit people to carry concealed firearms into bars, or anywhere else they want to. In Tennessee, over half a million people are licensed to carry a concealed weapon. Nashville-born novelist Madison Smartt Bell likes to say with a half smile that these kinds of permissive gun laws make for good manners: no one wants to make another person angry, because he or she might be armed.

A genuine honky-tonk might also display a Confederate flag stretched along the wall on which those armed white drinkers are leaning. Hardly a welcoming atmosphere for your standard middle-aged pair of tourists—or, for that matter, dark-skinned people, or LGBTQ people, or university students. Plenty of places do exist in Nashville to serve these and other clienteles, but to find them, or even to uncover a real honky-tonk, folks may have to go farther afield than Lower Broad. For many visitors, however, the raucous atmosphere of today's Lower Broad, with its crowds, cold beer, and live music, comes close enough to their idea of a honky-tonk that they go home satisfied.

In the postwar Nashville of my childhood, the place where sinners went Downtown to party was not Lower Broad, but a string of nightclubs and strip joints called Printer's Alley. The Alley, which thrived during the 1940s, '50s, and '60s, was, in fact, just that: a two-block-long alley running between Third and Fourth Avenues, where print shops were once located. At the height of its commercial activity in 1915, the Alley housed ten print shops, and thirteen publishers. A number of restaurants and saloons served the employees of these businesses.

Many of the saloons became speakeasies when Prohibition went into effect in Nashville in 1909, long before the rest of the nation. Prohibition ended in 1933, but not for Nashville. Patrons of the Alley's clubs brought their own booze in a brown paper bag, and bought high-priced mixers from the club's bar. Some of the best dancers/strippers in the Southeast performed in clubs such as The Rainbow Room and the Black Poodle Lounge. Sin was tucked away in the Alley, leaving the rest of the city with its strait-laced, Protestant facade intact. That was how Nashvillians generally preferred to treat the Devil's pleasures. A number of elegant gambling clubs existed in the 1950s, behind closed doors, which were patronized by the city's burghers. Some of the gambling clubs did not accept non-Christians as members, so Jews had their own. African Americans were not welcome in either kind, so they had their own places to gamble.

However, despite endless campaigns and legislation against moral turpitude, Nashville was no different from anywhere else human beings congregate, which is to say it was driven by Eros. It had its share of brothels, scandals, gay venues, and swingers' parties, but when I was growing up, anything that *publicly* deviated from the holy bonds of matrimony between a man and a woman was frowned on. Numerous self-appointed guardians of public morals were ever-ready to pounce and denounce.

For many Nashvillians, sin is acknowledged as a fact of life, but what is unforgivable is when the sin becomes public. We are all subject to temptation, but it should be kept private. Eros was kept under wraps except at places like the cheap "love" motels at the edge of town for heterosexuals, or the discreet, almost clandestine handful of bars catering to homosexuals. During the last half of the twentieth century, the local morning newspaper, *The Tennessean* (a daily newspaper that had published in the city under one name or another since 1812), periodically published the names of men arrested for soliciting sex from undercover policewomen posing as streetwalkers, or from male officers in park restrooms. This public shaming of the men arrested was a twentieth-century version of putting them in stocks. The fathers of kids my age were exposed to public opprobrium, and the kids suffered for the sins of their fathers. These lists in the morning newspaper were sometimes enough to tear a family apart, ruin a marriage, or drive a man to suicide.

Of course, love and its many relatives are the mainstays of Nashville's music, and Eros is almost always its driving energy. Country music is the white North American's version of the blues, speaking directly to the deep pleasures and sorrows of the flesh. Feelings hot and feelings cold, adultery, and abandonment are the staple subjects of Nashville's music, and for many people, this music is what defines the city.

The music industry in Nashville is not simply a machine to churn out "stars," but has long made the city one of the few places where a competent, working musician could find enough steady employment to feed a family and pay a mortgage. It is home to many members of the musicians' union who earn their keep playing with bands on the road, or doing back-up gigs in the recording studios. Nashville is also, traditionally, where the stars have their homes, and

Dolly Parton at the Opry, 2005.

where, in fact, they come *not to be* stars, but to relax and record when they are between tours. A famous singer is much more likely to be spotted in a restaurant or supermarket than on stage performing, and Nashvillians allow the stars their space, and time, to go about their lives, and to mingle with those of us who are just plain folks. Nevertheless, while headliners might not be much on offer, the city is full of excellent working musicians, and live music—country and other genres—is never far away.

The city's movers and shakers were never quite satisfied with Nashville being a second-tier city, more noted for its country music than for being an extraordinary place to live. Nashvillians considered themselves among God's fortunate elect, and wanted to boost the city to its rightful prominence, and prosperity. They have done so. In the twenty-first century, the collective dream of urban importance and sophistication has finally been realized. The city has been updated and globalized. But, at the same time, some Nashvillians worry that their city's relaxed charm is imperiled by so much growth and development. It is this struggle that defines the city today.

HISTORY

Alexander H. Wyant, *Tennessee*, 1866, oil on canvas.

1 Seven Hills and a River

For the centuries preceding the settlement of Nashville by Europeans, this Middle Tennessee landscape curving around a bend in the Cumberland River, and sheltered by seven adjoining hills, was known among Native American tribes for the riches of its woods and rivers. The area served as a regional breadbasket, hunted and fished by a number of tribes, including the Shawnee, Creek, Chickasaw, Cherokee, and Choctaw.

These tribes were not the original inhabitants of the Cumberland River basin. Before them had come the Mound Builders of the Mississippian Period, who are thought to have inhabited the area for centuries, from as early as 800 CE. Their history has been lost, however, and no one is sure why they disappeared so completely after about 1600. For decades, it was accepted that they had been nomadic, and not particularly developed, but recent archaeological discoveries seem to indicate that they organized sizeable cities. The Mississippians left behind few relics of their lives, but a great many related to their deaths: thousands of burial mounds across the Mississippi River network of territories, small hillocks rising above the landscape and holding the remains of their dead in stone-lined burial sites, along with various objects, which had obviously been dear enough to the deceased for them to be carried into the next world.

Even before the Mississippian period, people inhabited Middle Tennessee. The Woodland period began from perhaps as long ago as 1000 BCE. The people of this period were generally nomadic tribes, moving with the seasons: traveling, hunting, and trading. Over the centuries, many tribes made the shift from hunter-gatherers to farmers, and their civilization blended into that of the Mississippian. As this change progressed, more and more tribal members formed permanent settlements, leaving behind their nomadic way of life.

While Mississippians left behind few material artifacts, what evidence we have points to a complex, highly organized culture and social hierarchy. These structures were overwhelmed and eventually obliterated by the European colonists. In many parts of the New World, indigenous populations were entirely exterminated by diseases carried from Europe, and those who survived often perished from a long-rifle bullet.

As more and more land in Middle Tennessee, and across the Southeast, fell under the plough, many of the Mississippian burial mounds were scraped away and flattened, dug up, tilled, and planted. In some cases, foundations were laid on top of the flattened mounds, and houses were built upon them. Any relics that were unearthed might be put in a box in an attic or a shed, if the ploughman had a shred of sense, or simply tossed out with everything else broken and useless. The bones that turned up would be ploughed over and reburied, or carted away with the dirt, no respect paid to the dead. In fact, Nashville was built on so many of these levelled mounds that to this day, some Native Americans refer to it as the City of the Dead.

What initially attracted Europeans, and probably the Native Americans as well, was a salt lick by the river at the heart of what is now Downtown. It attracted a lot of game. One early explorer

Marine shell gorgets, 1250–1350 CE, recovered by William Myer (1862–1923) from Mound 1 at Castalian Springs, outside Nashville.

Female ancestor statue,
1000–1450 CE,
Mississippian art.

noted that you could walk across the backs of buffalo there for long distances without touching the ground. Herds of bison were said to roam Middle Tennessee, following a trail to the salt lick that is thought to have been close to present-day Dickerson Pike.

Various tribes used the riverine highway formed by Ohio Valley rivers such as the Cumberland for hunting, trade, and war. Native Americans moved a wide variety of goods along these rivers in a busy commercial trade, which included furs, food, and decorative shells. In the eighteenth century, according to historian John Egerton,

> it was understood among the various Indian tribes and the handful of French trappers and traders who ventured here that this park-like expanse of forest and streams could be hunted and fished by all, but possessed by none.

Bronze buffalo, Dickerson Pike, old bison trail.

However, not everything was peace and harmony. The tribes warred among themselves over territory, and in around 1714 the Cherokee and the Chickasaw expelled the Shawnee from Middle Tennessee. In the first years of the eighteenth century, a French trader took advantage of the commercial traffic along the Cumberland, establishing a trading post near the salt lick, and the place became known as French Lick, later Nashville. In the eighteenth century, the area had a particular attraction for French explorers and settlers. A trader named Jacques-Timothe de Montbrun frequented French Lick and later changed his name to Timothy Demonbreun. His first residence was a cave in a bluff beside the Cumberland River. In 1788 he settled permanently in Nashville, where he ran a tavern, as well as buying and selling merchandise.

Jane Thomas, who came to Nashville in 1804, wrote in her memoir,

> The first white man that ever lived in Nashville was named Demonbreun. He lived in a cave . . . There were two entrances to this cave, one on the river and one on the south side. He had three children born in the cave. He made his salt at the sulfur spring and hunted buffalo and deer that came there for water.

Alan LeQuire, bronze statue of Timothy Demonbreun, 1996, Riverfront Park.

Scalping

Both the colonists and the indigenous population liked to memorialize their battles by taking the scalps of their enemies. Even with all the game to be hunted, and the abundance of timber for building, those first Nashvillians had their hands full just to survive. It was not a new horror for James Robertson, who had seen scalping in North Carolina before leading settlers to Middle Tennessee. In a piece published in 1806 in the *Philadelphia Medical and Physical Journal*, he described the 1777 experience when he learned what to do for people who had been scalped, should they survive:

In March of the same year, Frederick Calvit was badly wounded, and nearly the whole of his head skinned. Doctor Vance was sent for, and staid several days with him. The skull bone was quite naked, and began to turn black in places, and, as Doctor Vance was about to leave Calvit, he directed me, as I was stationed in the same fort with him, to bore his skull as it got black, and he bored a few holes himself, to show the manner of doing it. I have found that a flat, pointed awl is the best instrument to bore with, as the skull is thick and somewhat difficult to penetrate. When the awl is nearly through, the instrument should be borne more lightly upon . . .

It will take, at least, two weeks from the time of boring for it to scale. When the scale is taken off at a proper time, all beneath it will appear flesh, like what we call proud-flesh, and as if there was no bone under it . . .

Robertson got a grisly opportunity to test out Dr. Vance's method when a companion at Fort Nashborough, David Hood, was shot and scalped.

In the year 1781, David Hood was shot, at this place [Nashville] with several balls, and two scalps were taken off his head, and these took off nearly all the skin which had hair on it. I attended him, bored his skull, and removed from almost the

Seth Eastman, *The Death Whoop*, 1849–55, watercolor.

whole of his head, such black scales as I have described above. It was three or four years before his head skinned over entirely; but he is now living, and is well . . .

I never knew one that was scalped, and bored as above directed, that did not perfectly recover. There is always part of the scalped head over which but little or no hair afterwards grows.

She was referring to a sulfur spring that was close by French Lick. The city's springs were gradually filled in, including the sulfur spring. It was buried under the vast, brick, Werthan Bag factory, constructed along Eighth Avenue North and finished in 1905, but a faucet was installed at one side of the building, which spouted sulfurous water from the spring when it was opened. Longtime Nashvillians believed the water to have curative powers, and up until the twenty-first century, it was not unusual to see people pull up to the sidewalk—sometimes in long, fancy cars—and get out with empty jugs to fill. The factory closed in 1995, and was converted into expensive Downtown condominiums in 2010. The faucet was removed and the pipe bricked over, cutting the city's last connection to the sulfur spring from which it sprang.

These low-lying springs of Jane Thomas's day were bounded by steep limestone bluffs, which are the primary geological formation in Nashville. Today's highways and interstates through the city are still bordered by these looming, layered, limestone bluffs. Caves abound. Two hundred million years ago, Middle Tennessee was covered by a shallow inland sea, and on the seabed were layers of shells. These formed the ubiquitous bluffs, tagging it with its nineteenth-century nickname: Rock City.

The novelist and historian Wilma Dykeman evoked pre-European Nashville:

This was limestone country to which the settlers and founders of Nashville came. Grasses and trees, animals and humans, the whole spectrum of life was influenced by this underlying foundation of the soil. Weather, too, played its role in the habitation of this place: extreme enough to permit the changing of the seasons but temperate enough to allow occasional mild interludes loosening winter's grip and refreshing periods of coolness relieving summer's heat.

The forests were the initial astonishment, as they had been in so many encounters with newcomers to the American land. Lofty, virgin, creating in their shade a sort of luminous green darkness even at midday, they dominated the landscape. To some

Fort Nashborough, First Ave. and Church St., Nashville, c. 1930–45, postcard.

of the settlers these forests represented "a howling wilderness" set in opposition to human civilization, a thing to be conquered and subdued as quickly as possible. To others, the forests were a welcome haven inviting exploration and understanding, a reserve to be used in the course of necessity and developing foresight.

In 1779 a small group of hunters and trappers made their way across the Great Smoky Mountains from North Carolina, led by James Robertson. At about the same time, John Donelson came by water, up the Cumberland River, and met with Robertson's party at a spot initially called the Bluffs. A small stockade was erected beside the Cumberland River and christened Fort Nashborough, in memory of a Revolutionary War general, Francis Nash.

The area surrounding the palisades was tremendously rich in game. One early hunting party of settlers reported that in five days, they had killed 105 bears, 75 buffalo, and 87 deer. It was not long before the settlers had exploited these resources almost to extinction. By 1800, buffalo were rarely, if ever, seen around Nashville.

Some of the fort's first residents lost their lives in the struggle to introduce the concept of private property to the indigenous tribes who had long considered this as common ground for the use of many and the ownership of none. They held that the rich land of Middle Tennessee belonged to everyone, in the same way as did air and water. The colonists wanted to divide it up among themselves. Gruesome atrocities were committed by both European settlers and Native Americans during the clash of cultures that erupted, including scalping, rape, and murder on both sides.

Despite its host of hardships and hostilities, the new settlement was directly in the path of westward expansion, and colonists continued to arrive. Almost from the outset, the town's founders imposed a strict moral code on inhabitants. The first to make regulations, enforce them, and make judicial rulings in disputes were the squires—those early European American settlers who each owned thousands of acres of land. Among the crimes that were prosecuted by these early courts were adultery; profane swearing; buying, selling, or grinding corn on the Sabbath; and bearing or siring children out of wedlock. In many of these cases, however, the record reflects courts that tended towards light punishment. Life in the frontier town was rugged and precarious, and a little moral turpitude was tolerated, and often practiced, by many of the early residents.

The historian Anita Shafer Goodstein, author of *Nashville, 1780– 1860: From Frontier to City*, wrote,

> The community was small enough to know intimately its neighbors' sins and determined enough to uphold standards of respectability by bringing those neighbors to court, but the squires were practical enough to punish lightly.

Shafer goes on to say that,

> Early Nashville experienced vivid instances of frontier individualism and chaotic breakdowns of order, but these were mitigated by the strong bonds of family, the relative homogeneity of the frontiersmen, and the rapid emergence of a leadership cadre that deliberately sought to maintain eighteenth century standards of law and deference.

Skirmishes with the indigenous populations became increasingly sporadic. In 1783 the Chickasaw chiefs signed a peace treaty with James Robertson and company, but the Cherokee and Creek tribes declined to do so. While increasing numbers of white settlers arrived with more arms, the Spanish were frequently accused of arming the indigenous tribes to help them attack English outposts. The last serious battle occurred in what is known as the Battle of the Bluffs, in 1792. An ambush was laid outside of Fort Nashborough's walls. Two Native American men approached the fort and drew attention and rifle fire. Some twenty white men came rushing outside and chased them, right into the jaws of an ambush by waiting warriors. A fierce battle erupted. Legend has it that James Robertson's wife loosed the fort's dogs, and that they drove the attackers back, allowing the white men time to retreat to the fort's safety. Five did not make it back, and an unrecorded number of Native Americans also died.

While this was the last real battle, a settler could never let down his or her guard outside the fort. Run-ins occurred, and people continued to die on both sides, but in 1794 a treaty was signed with the Cherokee Nation, and hostilities ended. Tennessee was admitted to the Union in 1796. A period of relatively peaceful coexistence between indigenous people and colonizers began, which permitted a more rapid expansion of the city.

By 1800 Nashville had 345 residents, including 136 slaves and fourteen free African Americans. The city limits had grown beyond the fort's walls, up the bluffs from the river. Businesses flourished around the public square: hotels, eating places, and boarding houses catered to the developing commercial life. In 1806 Nashville was incorporated as a city, and the county seat of Davidson County.

Andrew Jackson's Hermitage.

2 A Town Appears

It was a long time from 1779 and that first rough-hewn stockade on the river's banks, to 1812 and the construction of Andrew Jackson's luxurious manor called the Hermitage, a few miles outside of Nashville. The breadth of that change reflects the evolution of the city over its first four decades. Europeans had established hegemony, and no longer had reason to fear or fight Native Americans. They could concentrate on amassing wealth, and displaying it for all the world to see.

People could put their energies into making money instead of making war. Opportunities to prosper existed for both whites and free blacks. Among the fourteen free African Americans resident in Nashville in 1800 was a woman named Nell, who was a cook and baker; and Robert Renfro, who was legally a slave belonging to the settler Joseph Renfro, who himself was a slave before being emancipated. He opened a "house of entertainment" known as Black Bob's Tavern, close to the public square. In 1806 a free black man named Sherwood Brian settled in Nashville, and by 1850 he had amassed a considerable fortune, including 22 slaves of his own. Of course, these success stories were rare. Almost all the first and second generations of black people were slaves.

Their white masters used the same argument their descendants would use to justify segregation: blacks didn't have the qualities necessary to rise above their station, and they were happy with their lot and their treatment. The fact that such was not the case was illustrated by the frequent appearance of adverts in Nashville's newspapers such as this one from April 1832:

Ranaway from Nashville, on April 2, a mulatto girl named Paulina, belonging to Mr. J. B. Simpson. She is about 15 years of age, remarkably stout and strong for her age. She had on a pink spotted calico dress, a yellow handkerchief and a black one on her head, and took with her an old white frock and an old red calico one—Jervis Cutley, April 19, 1832.

Of the whites counted in that early census, only one hundred men and 35 women were older than sixteen. Many of these were not settled residents, but transients passing through for a longer or shorter period. Nevertheless, Nashville began to take on an identity of its own. Anita Shafer Goodstein wrote about the last decade of the eighteenth century:

During the nineties, the village had begun to acquire a physical center, the public square, four acres fronting on Water Street above the boat landing. On and around the square were clustered at least two of the town's taverns as well as artisans' sheds, lawyers' offices, merchants' warehouses, the courthouse, the jail, and the Masonic hall—all frame or log structures. Within

Alfred Jackson in his cabin. He was Andrew Jackson's slave and manservant until his master's death in 1845. Alfred Jackson died in 1901 at age 98.

what today must represent two or three short city blocks was concentrated an enormous amount of energy.

In 1797 a young Englishman named Francis Baily undertook a one-year journey through the unsettled parts of North America. He traveled some 2,000 miles (3,200 km) through territory largely inhabited by Native Americans, or not inhabited at all. He survived two shipwrecks, and on his return to London, became first a successful businessman, and later devoted himself to astronomy, becoming a fellow of the Royal Astronomical Society, and carrying out many scientific experiments. A crater on the Moon is named after him in recognition of his creation of an alloy.

In the book Baily wrote about his travels, *Journal of a Tour in Unsettled Parts of North America in 1796 and 1797,* he passed through Nashville, and his description was perhaps the first TripAdvisor review of the city:

> There are two or three taverns in this place, but the principal one is kept by Major Lewis. There we met a good fare, but very poor accommodations for lodgings: three or four beds of the roughest construction in one room, which was open at all hours of the night for any rude rabble that had a mind to put up at the house; and if the other beds were occupied you might be surprised in the morning to find a bedfellow by your side whom you have never seen before and perhaps might not see again.

He noted that Nashville consisted of "sixty to eighty" families, whose wage earners were mostly in business, and most of whom lived in houses that were "chiefly of log and frame." They burned easily. In December 1812 a raging fire would sweep through the village and destroy many of those houses. The citizens finally put out the flames using a bucket brigade to pass water up from the river to the burning buildings. From that point on, when Nashvillians had a choice, they chose to build brick homes.

As early as 1801, a board of commissioners was elected. Those qualified to vote were white males who owned at least one lot in town, or who had lived in Nashville for a minimum of six months. The first commissioners were three lawyers, a doctor, a newspaper editor, a shoemaker, and a tavern owner, who was also the village butcher and jailer. They promptly issued a set of rules for Nashville, which, at that point in time, had no police force, no paved streets, and no organized fire department. The rules stated that streets were to be kept clear of animal carcasses, businesses were to be closed on Sundays, and slaves were not allowed in bars, or to convene at homes after dark.

The town hired a watchman to walk the night-time streets and call out the hour. In her autobiography, *Old Days in Nashville* (1897), Jane Thomas remembered,

> After nine o'clock at night he used to walk up and down the streets and cry out the hours. If it was a rainy night, he would say: "Past eleven o'clock, a t'undering and a lightning, and a tam rainy night."

Women were relatively scarce in Nashville during that first decade of the nineteenth century. Those who were in residence were generally young—in 1800, 22 of the 35 adult white women counted in the census were between sixteen and 26. Youth counted for a lot, because the women in early Nashville generally had led rugged lives, and needed plenty of strength to bear them. Large families were the norm, and in addition to child-bearing, women's days were full of caring for those children, tending gardens and livestock, and preparing food for both immediate consumption and preservation. That was in addition to nursing the sick, and caring for anyone lucky enough to live to old age. Even with their hard lives, wives tended to outlive husbands, and widows often maintained themselves by keeping boarding houses or taverns.

Over the next few years, the village would begin to organize itself culturally, as well as logistically, and this work was often under the direction of female Nashvillians. Discussion societies, subscription libraries, reading rooms, amateur theater presentations, and debating societies were formed. Cumberland College was in place representing higher education, and the Nashville Female Academy opened in 1816 for the well-to-do daughters of farmers, merchants, and professional men. While itinerant preachers of various persuasions had passed through since the city's inception, it wasn't until 1812 that the first church—Presbyterian—was constructed. Religion was a sphere of daily life greatly shaped by women, and churches were also places where women were able to escape, for a brief time, from the heavy material demands and constraints of daily life.

Church served that same purpose for slaves, providing a place where they were not being watched and controlled by whites, where they could meet at least once a week in relaxed fellowship, as well as worship. It was about the only place where they were free to be themselves, because everywhere else they were objects, rather than humans.

Next to land and livestock, the most important possessions of early European American Nashvillians were their slaves. In the first twenty years as a community, more than seven hundred slaves were bought and sold, and the volume of sales only increased as the city grew. Slaves often worked from "sun to sun" during the week on a schedule that did not allow for more than an animal existence: work, eat, and sleep. Sunday was the week's only day of rest, when they could gather together at church. Slaveholding was by no means limited to field work. In the city itself, merchants and craftsmen often had slave labor doing the heavy lifting in their places of business.

However, the town's growth also meant more black residents—both slave and free—and more opportunities for socializing. Places catering to blacks like so-called "houses of entertainment" and tipling shops erected on the highway caused frequent consternation among the white populace, and in 1823 a Sunday patrol was instituted to assure that black residents behaved themselves on the Lord's day.

Nashville is on the New Madrid Fault Line, and suffered a series of earthquakes beginning in 1811, the first in a long line of natural disasters that would strike the city, and still continue to do so. And also as it still continues to do, the city recovered and moved on. By 1816 Nashville was a thriving market hub, serving the tobacco

Fort Marr Blockhouse, near Benton, Tennessee, the last surviving remnant of the forts used to intern the Cherokee, in preparation for their forced removal west on the Trail of Tears in the 1830s.

Indians Emigrating, wood engraving, depicting the removal of the Cherokees to the West in 1838 in the typical textbook fashion of the time: Native Americans as well-fed "emigrants," when in fact they were on a forced march into exile, during which many thousands died of hunger, sickness, and cold.

Cherokee

The Cherokee tribes were driven from their ancestral lands in Middle Tennessee by Andrew Jackson's resettlement decree. An October 1838 article by C. C. Norvell in the *Nashville Whig* newspaper described one group:

The second detachment of the emigrating Cherokees passed through Nashville Monday on their way to the "Far West." They lay encamped near Foster's Mill on the Murfreesboro Turnpike for several days, and while there were visited by many of our citizens. We had no opportunity of seeing this miserable remnant of a warlike race in camp; but a worthy subscriber residing in the country, writes that he was present several times, and regrets to say that many of the Indians appeared extremely needy in apparel. Barefooted and badly clad, they cannot all hope to withstand the fatigues of travel and the inclemency of the season. Disease and perhaps death must be the portion of scores of their number before they reach the Western frontier. Indeed four or five were buried near town, and not less than 50 were on the sick list when they passed through Monday. The same correspondent asks us to propose to our fellow citizens some means of relief . . . but we confess our inability to do so, beyond suggesting the propriety and humanity of contributing such donations of clothing &c. as might be conveniently spared and would be of real service to the recipients. In this way the ladies— always first in works of charity, could do much to alleviate the sufferings of our red brethren.

We understand that a minister of the gospel accompanies each detachment, through whom all donations of clothing could be judiciously distributed.

and cotton farmers of Middle Tennessee. By 1820 the city's black population had grown six times greater than in 1800, and the white population was eleven times greater than in 1800. It was predominantly male, with two men for every woman in the white adult population. This encouraged the creation of more boarding houses, in which a man, or two men, rented a room, and received their meals.

The town was booming with more people arriving every week. In 1826 Nashville was named the state capital, relocating from Murfreesboro. Even the collapse of the cotton market in 1819 was not enough to do more than temporarily slow down commercial activity. It was also in 1819 when the first of many steamboats docked at the foot of Lower Broad. Business opportunities were constantly increasing. Population growth occurred even in spite of the fact that over the course of a decade, some 70 percent of the city's residents moved on, so it is evident that Nashville was drawing a steady flow of newcomers.

Not everyone left. Those who stayed were often those who already had substantial holdings of property, and a number of the city's most important leaders were descendants of those first Fort Nashborough settlers. This later generation was often made up of professionals: lawyers, doctors, bankers, or farmers with holdings of thousands of acres. The politicians and policymakers who rose from their ranks generally served the interests of these professionals, in combination with those of the large merchants.

Nashvillians no longer felt they were living in a frontier village. Rather, they envisioned a civilized, sophisticated, cultured city. In 1817 the Abercrombie family opened Nashville's first real school, the Belmont Domestic Academy for young ladies. The master of the house taught French, music, and dancing, while his wife taught literature, and their two daughters assisted with whatever needed to be done. Jane Thomas recalled them as "very elegant and accomplished people." The daughters of the city's most prosperous families were enrolled.

Family connections were already important in Nashville, and the foundations of a good-old-boy network were laid down, connections that would still mean something in the twenty-first century.

First Presbyterian Church, 154 Fifth Avenue, 20th-century photograph. Designed in 1849 by William Strickland, architect for the State Capitol, the building was completed in 1851. It is representative of the Egyptian style of architecture with Egyptian columns and moldings. Once Nashville's largest building, it was used as a hospital and stables during the Civil War.

Copy after Charles Bird King, *Spring Frog, A Cherokee Chief, c.* 1838. Born on the north side of Chickamauga Creek at the edge of Lookout Mountain near Chattanooga, Tennessee, in 1754, Spring Frog was an excellent naturalist and aided John James Audubon on his excursions through the Tennessee region.

In addition to landholding, the profession of law was particularly appealing to a number of those early Nashvillians. Some of the lawyers went to work for the growing body of merchants, writing contracts and collecting debts. Others were retained by banks, and still others dealt in land disputes. In 1823 the local newspaper had advertisements for legal services from 26 different lawyers practicing in town.

Andrew Jackson was both a part of and not a part of this good-old-boy network of lawyers. Born in modest circumstances in 1767, he became a frontier lawyer who advanced to be a justice on the state's Supreme Court, then a lauded general in the War of 1812, and finally President of the United States. His sympathies were with the well-to-do, but his early life meant that he was also constantly aware of the struggles of the hardworking farmers and clerks who came to see in him the ideals of a true democracy. Jackson was himself a slave-holder. He was staunchly anti-Native American and pro-expansion.

As president, he encouraged, and in 1830 oversaw, the beginning of years of merciless forced removal of tribes from the Southeast to lands across the Mississippi, the most blatant of ethnic cleansings. Native Americans were banished from their ancestral lands, forced to walk in appalling conditions along the trail now known as the Trail of Tears to the Native American territories west of the Mississippi River. Some 4,000 people died making the journey.

Tennessee's tribes had roots in the land that stretched back for centuries. They had a cultural heritage deeply entwined with a knowledge of their Middle Tennessee world, a social organization and way of life that had been passed down through many generations. The Cherokee language is thought to be more than 3,000 years old, and in the 1820s, a tribal member named Sequoyah created a syllabary for it, converting it into a written language. Cherokee is still spoken by some 2,000 people.

The land left behind by the various expelled tribes released a great deal more land for farming cotton and tobacco, and for other

Ralph Eleaser
Whiteside Earl,
Andrew Jackson,
1835, oil on canvas.

money-making ventures in Jackson's home state. Property meant money then, just as it does today. Nowhere was this newly vacated land more appreciated than in Jackson's hometown. Nashville was evolving into a prosperous city, a transportation and mercantile hub. By 1855 the population had grown to more than 10,000. It had street lights, and a medical school had opened at the University of Nashville. Steamboat traffic was constant on the river, and the fastest vessels could reach New Orleans in six days. Hundreds of miles of roads led in and out of the city, and railroads had begun to connect it with the rest of the country.

Nashville also had a vibrant cultural life. By 1819, an old salt warehouse had been repurposed as a theater, and featured both local and touring productions. The city had some of the best bookstores in the Southeast. In 1844 Ralph Waldo Emerson wrote in a letter that Nashville was second only to Boston in the sale of his books. Of course, many Nashvillians never read a book in their lives once they left school, assuming that they attended school in the first place. The most popular entertainment was when a traveling circus came to town, and excitement began to mount when the first posters went up announcing the coming event. Tickets were cheap, and it was something to be enjoyed by an entire family.

Unknown artist, *Nashville*, lithograph depicting a steamboat going down the Cumberland River, and the city perched on a hill, 1855–9.

Ralph Waldo Emerson's books were bestsellers in Nashville. Lithograph by Leopold Grozelier, 1859.

More refined offerings were also well received. In the early 1850s, a new Downtown theater named the Adelphi was built, where touring companies offered everything from Shakespeare to grand opera. Nashvillians, concerned that their city be seen to be every bit as culturally important as Boston or New York, convinced P. T. Barnum, the most important promoter of his day, to book two Adelphi appearances by superstar Jenny Lind on her 1850–52 tour of the nation. Barnum agreed to add Nashville to the tour on condition that the seating capacity of the Adelphi be increased so it would hold 1,700 people. It was done. Barnum came to Nashville and inspected the Adelphi. He pronounced himself satisfied and tickets went on sale. While the tickets were generally thought to be expensive, at between $3–$12, both seating and standing room for the concert were sold out.

Life among the well-to-do had its own entertainments. The social calendars of Nashville's better families were full of parties, balls and "dinings," which were evenings spent eating and later socializing in the drawing room, lubricated by a good deal of wine and whiskey.

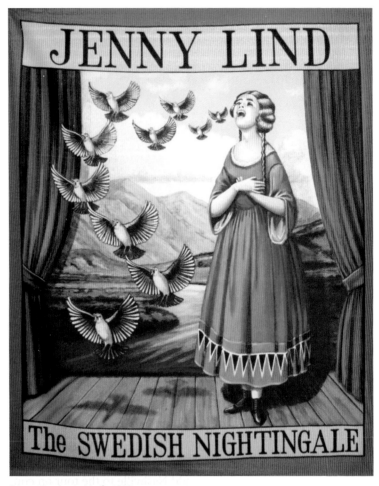

Advert for Jenny Lind's 1850 tour.

The standard menu at these evening soirées was ample: beginning with soup and rice; moving on to fish with potatoes, a whole boiled ham, roast beef, turkey, many vegetables, and a wide choice of dessert; and after the guests were done, the help was allowed to divvy up what remained. Jane Thomas remembered,

> What was left was given to the servants, and the amount given to them was much greater and much nicer than is prepared now to feed fifty or a hundred people at the parties. At the

dinings they had the greatest abundance of everything: meats, vegetables, jellies, and desserts. Boiled puddings of all kinds, with rich sauce, were a favourite dessert.

Nashvillians congratulated themselves on their level of cultural attainment, even before the Jenny Lind concerts. John Egerton noted in *Nashville: The Faces of Two Centuries, 1780–1980*,

> One historian of the period, writing on Nashville's cultural life, characterized the city in 1850 as having "much unwarrantable pretension" and a "tendency to boast and to exaggerate." Pretension—or at least cockiness—must have been almost irresistible for the mixture of people who in three generations had built a city on a wilderness bluff.

They had reason to be proud. The city they built had antebellum mansions, paved sidewalks, and a bustling commercial life for its 10,000 or so inhabitants. The city's port and wharf, at the bottom of Broadway, was a hive of economic activity. Merchants and warehouses served the river traffic, and as many as nine steamboats a day docked, discharging people and goods. An English traveler to Nashville, G. W. Featherstonhaugh, wrote in his *Excursion through the Slave States, from Washington on the Potomac to the Frontier of Mexico* (1844),

> The first log-hut ever erected in Nashville was in 1780; now here is a handsome town, good substantial brick houses, with public edifices that would embellish any city in America . . . Besides these there are numerous extensive warehouses, evidences of a brisk commerce, and an exceedingly well constructed bridge thrown across the Cumberland River.

Daguerreotype of President James K. Polk and Sarah Childress Polk by John Plumbe's studio, Washington, DC, c. 1848–9, shortly before he died in Nashville of cholera.

3 A War Zone

Not all the consequences of Nashville's growth were positive. No longer a village, but rather a small city, it had its share of urban problems. Waterborne diseases were more easily transmitted among the population. A cholera epidemic in 1849 swept through Nashville and claimed many lives, including that of James K. Polk, who was only three months out of office as the eleventh president of the United States, and had returned to live at his Nashville mansion when cholera cut him down. W. F. Cooper, a Nashvillian who lived through the epidemic, wrote to a friend, days after Polk's death, "Fully two hundred deaths have occurred in the last fortnight—nearly half of them during the three last days. On Friday there were 38 burials, on Saturday 41, and on Sunday about 15."

In fact, it would be decades before good health was established in the community, and it was unusual to live to an old age in the first half of the nineteenth century. Coal was the principal fuel, and a pall often hung over the city from the coal smoke generated by fires in homes and factories. Summers were tremendously humid and winters were cold and damp. Sanitation and hygiene were still impossible for many.

In addition to the generally poor quality of public health, other problems began to surface. As Nashville prospered, it attracted more and more immigrants, most of them young men looking for work. The American Revolution had slowed immigration way down, and until around 1830, numbers stayed low. But there were always some "native" Nashvillians who saw newly arrived foreigners as threats to both the job market and their daughters. One strike against the immigrants was the usual cry that they were robbing jobs from "the natives." Another was that they were primarily from Ireland and Germany, and the majority of them were Catholics. Nashville had already defined itself as a Protestant city. The poor living conditions of the immigrants, crowded into neighborhoods of slums and shanties, only confirmed the low opinion in which they were held by many of the city's more respectable citizens. In 1850 only a handful of Jews—"five families and eight young men"—were counted, but by 1860 there were 105 Jewish households and their community was continuing to grow.

While Nashvillians worried about the increasing number of foreigners, a darker cloud was approaching, one that presented a graver threat to the city than disease or immigration: the Civil War. Egerton wrote of 1860 Nashville in *Face of Two Centuries* that it was

> a new city, and it had the rough edges to prove it—it had conspicuous opulence cheek by jowl with abject poverty; it had dirty air and dirty water and muddy streets; it could count sixty-nine houses of prostitution . . . It may have needed refinement and reform, but it did not need war.

Racial tensions grew as the abolitionist movement made itself increasingly felt among black and white alike. The presidential election of 1856 generated intense emotions on both sides of the question. Recurrent rumors of imminent slave insurrections kept people of both races on edge. Free black Nashvillians were increasingly vilified by the white media. A school for free blacks, in existence since 1839, was permanently closed by vigilantes, and city authorities. In December 1856, white native Nashvillians joined forces with recent white immigrants to the city, and attacked free blacks, who were supposedly taking their jobs, and the bread from the mouths of their families. Two dozen blacks were jailed after the riot, but were later released. Numerous black, free families left the city for more hospitable places.

War proved unavoidable, and Nashville was on the wrong side, choosing to defend its established order, just or unjust. Slavery was as much a fact of life in the city as in the fields around it, and slave labor was an important contributing factor to its prosperity. While Nashville and the surrounding Davidson County were not generally home to plantation owners with large slave holdings, many white people both in town and in the country owned a few slaves. In 1860 more than one-third of Nashville's households owned at least one enslaved black person, according to Anita Shafer Goodstein, and they were bought and sold at Nashville's market house.

We have a description of a slave sale there one New Year's Day. It was written by a black barber, a Nashvillian named James P. Thomas (1827–1913), a former slave who became a successful businessman. His mother was a slave, and his father was a white man, John Catron, who was later a u.s. Supreme Court justice. In Thomas's autobiography, written during his last years, he wrote of his father, "He presided over the Supreme Court ten years but he had no time to give me a thought. He gave me 25¢ once. If I was correctly informed that was all he ever did for me."

Thomas was a fascinating person, who had many interests. He was legally freed by his master in 1851, after years of barbering in his own shop close to Nashville's public square. In 1856 he turned up in Nicaragua to help another Nashvillian, William Walker, who had been installed as the president of that country, and was attempting to unite the various nations of the region. Thomas became quickly disillusioned when he learned that the white Walker wanted to institute slavery in his new fiefdom, and he returned to the States in 1857. William Walker was later exiled from Central America. When he tried to return, he was arrested and executed.

Thomas decided to try his luck as a land speculator in Missouri, where he prospered, eventually opening a luxurious barber shop, owning numerous rental properties, and becoming one of the richest black men in the United States. His fortune was wiped out, however, by bad investments and the market crash of 1893. He lived to the age of 89, dying in 1913 and having been reduced to ending his life in a rundown two-room apartment in Saint Louis.

In his autobiography, Thomas remembers and describes the fear of having their families torn apart that many slaves in Nashville had to live with every day:

It was a common thing to know nothing about what was going on until a strange man would come and say, "I've bought you. Come with me." I have known cases where a child was sold to punish the mother. Others would sell the mother and keep the child.

Less than two years before the outbreak of the terrible Civil War, life was good for many free white Nashvillians. They lived in a growing, prosperous city. A travel piece about making a journey on the Louisville and Nashville Railroad ran in the *Louisville Journal* in October 1859:

> It was after five o'clock before we reached Nashville, and in the golden flood of the sunset it presented a beautiful appearance—the new Capitol, the most conspicuous object in the distance, and the suspension bridge over the Cumberland River, poised in airy lightness like a telegraph wire . . .
>
> Nashville possesses a great many fine stores and palatial residences, but very many of the citizens occupy cottage houses, a few miles from the turmoil of business. The Lebanon turnpike is filled with these suburban abodes. The press is an institution in Nashville. There are five daily newspapers, and the editorial corps is distinguished.

For all its pretensions to greatness, there are times in the life of a city, as in the life of a person, when it is best to be unimportant and unremarkable. Unfortunately, that was not the case for Nashville as war approached. The city had considerable strategic importance for the Confederate forces. The Louisville and Nashville railroad was the only one covering both Union and Confederate territory. Nashville had several arms factories, which supplied the Confederate army. Its status as a transportation hub meant that the Union wanted it neutralized and under Yankee control.

Still, Nashvillians considered themselves well protected by the garrison of Confederate soldiers in residence, and by the upriver fortifications of Fort Donelson, which they trusted were sufficient to repel any Yankee incursions. When the news arrived that federal gunboats had swept past the fort and were on their way towards Nashville, the "Rebel", Confederate, leaders decided that they were outgunned and outnumbered, and opted for a strategic retreat. Nashville became the first major city in the South to fall to Union forces, and it fell without a fight, surrendering to the oncoming Union army in February 1862, with the Rebel forces in full retreat from the city. Virtually overnight, Nashvillians, who had counted on being defended by the soldiers in gray, had to adjust to a hostile army in their midst, where it stayed until the end of the war in 1865.

Jane Thomas had her house confiscated to quarter the occupying forces, and had to pay rent in her own home in order to occupy two rooms. Years later, she recalled,

> A Yankee named Heeley and his wife had a room here part of the time. He was the grandest thief I ever saw . . . He stole all the clothes for his wife to wear, and she had seven stolen breast-pins. They went foraging every day, and came back with all kinds of things. There was one man named Treat who used my servant's room to put his stolen goods in. His wife was here with him, and she ate and associated with the negroes all the time.

Bombardment and capture of Fort Henry by the federal gunboats under the command of Commodore Andrew H. Foote, February 6, 1862.

A. E. Matthews, "The First Union Dress Parade in Nashville,"
March 4, 1862.

Lizzie Hardin

Nashvillians had to accustom themselves to living under Yankee occupation, with few ways to offer any resistance. In February 1862 Lizzie Hardin was a Nashville teenager from a pro-Confederate family, and in her diary, published a century later as *The Private War of Lizzie Hardin: A Kentucky Confederate Girl's Diary of the Civil War*, she recorded the city's shocking surrender before the oncoming Union forces:

> When I crossed the bridge and reached the square in Nashville I beheld a city upon which the foe was advancing. Those who once witnessed such a scene need no description. To those who have not, no description can give any idea of its wild confusion. The streets were filled with carriages, horses, buggies, wagons, drags, carts, everything which could carry a human being from the doomed city . . . Every store and every shop was closed while the people refused to be seen even at the doors or windows of private residences. The Yankees in the most magnificent uniforms, and with bands which made the city echo to hostile airs, march through the streets tormented and enraged as only a Yankee can be by a total failure to make any impression on the contemptuous Southerners. When on the street we turned our eyes from them when possible, or followed them with looks of silent malediction . . . We had no pleasure but in insulting our oppressors, but we did not stint ourselves in that.

During the Civil War, the Planter's Hotel housed soldiers and served as a military hospital, 1865, photograph.

Suddenly, life was not so easy. The prices of food and clothing shot up, when they were available. The Union army took what it needed from the civilian population, and left Nashvillians struggling with chronic shortages. Things once taken for granted such as sugar and flour became hard to find. In addition, the presence of so many uniformed young men represented a threat to the morals of the city's young women, particularly because eligible young male Nashvillians were either being held as prisoners, or had retreated with the Confederate ranks.

Because it was occupied so rapidly, and without a shot being fired inside the city, Nashville was spared any bloody battles during the first two years that the Yankees were in residence, although the war brought plenty of other tribulations. In addition to the scarcity of life's necessities, emancipated slaves from the countryside arrived in great numbers, seeking refuge and living hand-to-mouth in the most rudimentary shelters. Wounded and captured Confederate soldiers were allowed to return home on the proviso that they refrain from taking up arms again.

By the end of the war, Nashville's population had swollen to some 80,000. Crime skyrocketed, and Confederate spies and saboteurs were scattered across the crowded city. Tensions were high, as Nashvillians were forced to accept Union soldiers billeted in their homes and eating from their larders. Prostitution thrived. In 1863 military authorities arrested 150 prostitutes and put them on a steamboat headed upriver. They were promptly returned by authorities in Louisville and Cincinnati. Numerous buildings were requisitioned to serve as military hospitals. One former school was turned into a hospital treating only cases of venereal disease.

Scene in the yard of a military hospital in Nashville, showing numerous men and women, some African American, among lines of hanging laundry, July 1863. This may have been a house of prostitution.

Resources were few, but at least there was no fighting—until, that is, December 1864, only a few months before the war's end, when Confederate forces made a desperate attempt to retake the city and were routed in the two-day Battle of Nashville, in which thousands were killed and wounded. War was a spectator sport in those days, and Nashvillians watched it from their rooftops, and from atop the hills overlooking the battlefields, which encompassed much of the city.

One of the ways that Union forces stationed in Nashville had kept busy over the intervening years was by constructing defensive works around the city. By the time the Confederate Army tried to overrun them, they encountered a well-entrenched force. The weather was bitterly cold. The Cumberland River protected North and East Nashville from attack, while fierce fighting raged for two days throughout West and South Nashville. It was to be the last battle west of the coastal states, a decisive victory for the Union, which virtually ended Confederate military efforts in Tennessee.

A number of sites still exist that played a role in the battle. The stately Downtown First Presbyterian Church served as a hospital, and Fort Negley was one of the redoubts constructed to repulse a

Kurz & Allison, *Battle of Nashville*, c. 1891, chromolithograph.

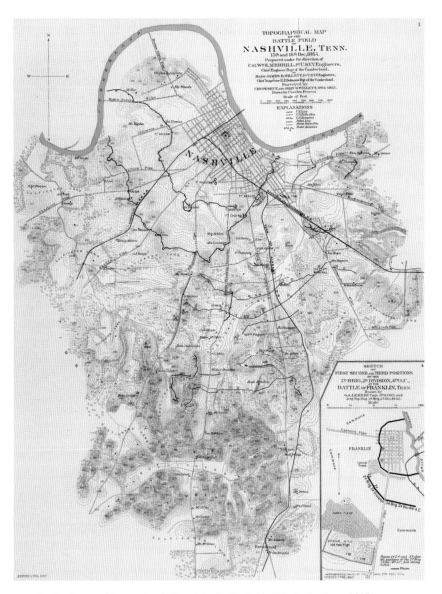

Charles Peseux, *Topographical Map of the Battle Field of Nashville, Tenn.*, 1895.

Confederate charge—African Americans, many of whom were still legally enslaved, were conscripted to build it. A 55-acre (22 ha) park was built around the fort in the late 1930s. In 2016 plans were announced to develop it into prime Downtown real estate, a plan that was eventually shelved due to opposition from historical preservationists.

Less than five months on from the Battle of Nashville, an armistice was signed and the war was over. Nashvillians could get back to doing what they did best: making money. Despite the hard times brought by the war, once the aftermath of the clean-up and homecoming of soldiers was done, the city found itself with opportunities that would help it recover, and knit itself back together. In addition to the numerous former slaves who had come to the city from the country, and the returning Confederate soldiers, many of the Union troops who spent the war occupying Nashville had met and married women there, and decided to remain after the armistice was signed. More than 170 Union soldiers married while they were stationed in Nashville, including at least thirteen high-ranking Union officers who married Nashville women and settled down in the city after the war. Life was certainly not easy through the early years after the Civil War, but its aftermath found an increasingly diverse population willing and eager to adjust to the new realities.

4 Reconstruction and Recovery

U nlike other southern cities such as Mobile, Alabama, or Charleston, South Carolina, where the Civil War's devastation delayed recovery for many years, it did not take long for Nashville to rebuild, regroup, and reignite its entrepreneurial energy. The same traits that had made it such an attractive prize for the Union at the start of the war now served as a foundation on which to build a stable, thriving economy.

Principal among the opportunities was the railroads. As it had been for steamboats, and would later be for long-haul truck traffic, Nashville was at a strategic location to serve as a transportation hub. And the railroads opened the nation to those fields where Nashvillians excelled: manufacturing, wholesale trade, finance, printing, and publishing. It soon became evident that steamboats were in decline. While the railroads increased revenues from year to year, the annual tonnage moved by steamboats fell precipitously.

By 1870 the economic and social recovery was in full swing, although there were some setbacks during those first postwar years. In 1866, and again in 1873, cholera outbreaks killed nearly a thousand people in each epidemic. In addition to disease, wrote John Egerton in *Face of Two Centuries*,

> A general condition of unplanned and uncoordinated growth prevailed . . . Social and economic class divisions were unimproved if not more pronounced. The few blacks who gained a measure of wealth or influence were as susceptible to corruption as whites, and for the multitude of the poor and unskilled

and illiterate of both races, conditions of health, and life were in some ways worse than ever. To all this could be added the frightening presence of the Ku Klux Klan, a secret organization of ex-Confederate vigilantes who carried out night-riding acts of intimidation and terrorism for several years after the war.

Despite these ups and downs, the city healed. The important suspension bridge across the Cumberland, which had opened in 1850 to great fanfare at the site of today's Woodland Street Bridge, was destroyed by the Confederates as they fled the city in 1862. By 1866 a new one was in place, and that same year, mule-drawn street-cars were introduced in the city's streets. This made possible a move towards the outskirts, because people who moved out to these first suburbs could be connected by the streetcars to Downtown. It was the beginning of a "white flight" that would last 150 years, facili-tated by internal combustion engines and improved roads, until the twenty-first century, when white Nashvillians began moving back to the inner city.

Even as the postwar economy grew, and commercial Downtown expanded, a lot of people aspired to move further away from the city center. At the same time as the fancy new Maxwell House Hotel was opened Downtown in 1869—good enough eventually to host seven presidents, from Andrew Johnson to Woodrow Wilson—pre-viously undeveloped land at the far end of those streetcar tracks was increasing in value and desirability. A lot of the economic activ-ity Downtown came from foundries, factories, and slaughterhouses, which combined to produce a sooty, bad-smelling, miasmic air, to say nothing of the contribution made by human waste. As late as 1898, the city counted only 682 indoor toilets, 212 bathtubs and 52 urinals among a population of more than 80,000.

While Downtown provided easy access to public offices, ware-houses, and the river port, a ring of slums had grown up on the periphery of the business district, including numerous barely livable shacks on the western and northern slopes of Capitol Hill, directly beneath the State Capitol building, where they would continue until the mid-twentieth century. Taverns and brothels were concentrated

Maxwell House Hotel, *c.* 1925.

Downtown. Inhabited by Irish or German immigrants, and former slaves, the densely populated slums were also refuges for criminals and miscreants. Seventy-two percent of black Nashvillians lived within eight blocks of the public square. Sanitary conditions were virtually nonexistent; tuberculosis and pneumonia thrived in the slums. Longtime Nashvillians identified the epicenters of the periodic cholera outbreaks to these insalubrious neighborhoods, although this was not necessarily the case.

In stark contrast to the shanties were the postwar mansions built by Nashville's aristocracy. Palatial homes such as Belmont and Riverwood were built outside of the city on large tracts of land, constituting the top rung in a rigid social hierarchy. However, the great majority of Nashvillians lived neither in the slums of Black Bottom, nor in the opulent homes of Belle Meade. Most lived in modest houses and maintained their families with their hard-won wages.

Medical advances came slowly, but gradually doctors amassed an inventory of effective remedies. Morphine was discovered before the Civil War, but not generally used as an analgesic until it proved itself on the battlefield, and in short order came to be used, and abused, widely. Jane Thomas wrote of one such case that happened at a party she attended:

> Mrs Blood, a very fascinating woman, was at the party. They had just begun inhaling morphine [in Nashville]. She had a headache and someone advised her to take morphine. She took it and was overpowered. They had to get a couch and put her on it . . . Mrs Barrow asked me to go and see what to do for her. When I went in to her she was hysterical, and said, "O Miss Jane, will I die?" I said: "O no, Mrs Blood; you will be all right in a few minutes" . . . After that she was always a dear friend of mine, and never came to Nashville that she did not come to see me.

Capitol Hill, pre-urban renewal, 1950s.

Riverwood Mansion, August 1940, photo by Lester Jones.

Electric streetcars replaced those pulled by mules, and increased the city's potential for expansion. The animals could only pull along relatively flat routes, and had proven costly to maintain. Electric-powered streetcars made it possible for young couples with families to settle in the suburbs, even if they weren't making a lot of money. In fact, many of the same investors who put money into the new streetcars were also heavy promoters of suburban tracts. Land was not too expensive, and the building trades flourished until the 1893 market crash, which slowed the pace of prosperity. By that time, Nashville was irrevocably committed to suburban living.

While there were two economic downturns and market collapses from 1865 to 1900, for the majority of those years, Nashville was an attractive place for people to live and do business. It also became a center of education for both black and white students. Fisk University opened in 1866 as a college that prepared African

Cholera

Both Vanderbilt University and Meharry Medical College would eventually graduate thousands of doctors, and in the city itself, good doctors were sorely needed. Sanitary conditions were far from ideal. A 1938 book titled *The Conquest of Cholera*, by J. S. Chambers, described the conditions that underlay the 1873 cholera epidemic, which killed an estimated 1,000 Nashvillians. He concluded that the epidemic's origins were more likely to lie with the mansions than with the slums:

> At Nashville the scourge found things favorable for a bountiful harvest of deaths . . . Waste of every kind, accumulated in the streets, alleys, and back yards, were of such a character as to offend all of one's senses not dulled by constant exposure to them.
>
> Human waste was received in various types of outhouses, the almost universal custom of the time. In the lowlands along the creeks where resided the poorer classes, the privies were of the surface or shallow pit kinds whose contents were washed with every rain into the creeks. But the senses of the elite of the city, living on the hill, were offended by the foul accumulations of the surface toilets and their individual resourcefulness and genius found a way; they blasted holes into the limestone and the more fortunate obtained pits which opened into underground streams or caverns . . . And some of the oldest residences boasted privies that had never been cleaned and had always remained "sweet and unoffensive." It had occurred to no one that these same underground streams might feed the numerous springs and wells under the hills which supplied the water for those districts.

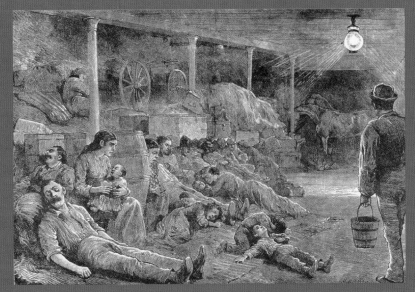

Matt (Somerville) Morgan, "Victims of cholera on a steamboat traveling on the Mississippi River," from *The Cholera Epidemic of 1873 in the United States* (1875).

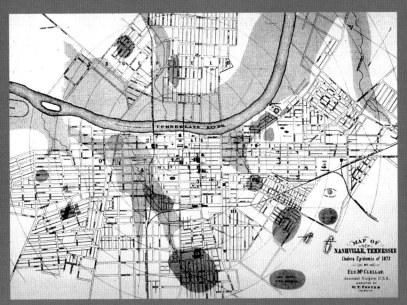

Map of the cholera epidemic of 1873 in Nashville, by Ely McClellan, Assistant Surgeon.

American teachers. Only five years after it opened, a cash-flow crisis threatened to close its doors. An a cappella singing ensemble, the Fisk Jubilee Singers, was formed by the school's treasurer and music director. The group toured the country raising funds, and eventually were invited to perform in Europe and Japan. Fisk expanded into a university well before the end of the century, but it would not have an African American president until 1947, long after it had become one of the most prestigious black universities in the South.

In 1876 a medical college opened, which would become Meharry Medical College, the first medical school to train black physicians in the Southeast. The school was named after its primary benefactor, a white Scots-Irish salt trader named Samuel Meharry, who was rescued and cared for by a group of free African Americans in the 1820s when his wagon fell into a swamp. In gratitude, he promised he would one day do something for their race. Decades later, in 1875, he and his four brothers donated $30,000 to establish the medical school.

On the other side of town, the autumn of 1875 inaugurated the first academic year for Vanderbilt University, which opened with

Studio group portrait of the Fisk Jubilee Singers, c. 1872. Left to right: Minnie Tate, Greene Evans, Isaac Dickerson, Jennie Jackson, Maggie Porter, Ella Sheppard, Thomas Rutling, Benjamin Holmes, and Eliza Walker.

Old Gymnasium, Vanderbilt University, 2010.

some three hundred white students in attendance, and had twice that many by 1900. The university was established with an endowment of $500,000 from Cornelius Vanderbilt, a shipping and railroad magnate, who was then the richest man in the nation.

Within a decade after the war, Nashville was the fourth largest city in the Southeast, drawing white and black alike. In 1860, 25 percent of the city's residents were black, but ten years later, that had risen to 38 percent. People newly emancipated from slavery poured into the city, looking for work in the recovering economy. By the 1880s, an educated black middle-class had developed, but segregation was the norm. African Americans were generally left in the central city, and those who managed to move out built their nice homes in North Nashville near Fisk and Meharry, literally across the railroad tracks from the white neighborhoods. They still suffered segregation, but they suffered it in neighborhoods that were newer, more organized, and less polluted than the inner city.

Schools were organized by race, as were churches, hospitals, and public facilities. The resident minorities—Jews, Roma, and African

Americans—had little voice in the urban planning process. They were expected to keep their heads down, work hard, and abide by the will of the white Protestants. The densest concentration of African Americans was in the neighborhood called "Black Bottom," south of Lower Broad. The name derived not from the color of the people who lived there, but from the black mud and fetid pools of water that were always present, due to the frequent overflow from the Cumberland River. Those who could afford to do so moved out of the bottomlands, but their options were limited, with white neighborhoods closed to them.

African Americans were "the other," and were never allowed to forget it. Between 1890 and 1950, at least 204 black men were lynched by mobs in Tennessee. They were not the only despised minority. The mere mention of "Gypsies" also inspired fear and indignation among the solid white citizens. A large number of Irish Travelers, who were not Roma but shared their lifestyle, had buried their dead at Calvary Cemetery in Nashville since the nineteenth century. They gathered to say a funeral Mass for the previous year's dead every May 1 at St Patrick's Catholic Church, in East Nashville. Hundreds of Irish Travelers from all across the Southeast came to visit the cemetery and celebrate the Mass, much to the dismay of the citizenry.

An 1893 city ordinance read,

> No person or persons shall be permitted, directly or indirectly, within the limits of this city, to exercise the business of fortune-telling, or to propose or attempt to tell fortunes, or do anything pertaining thereto, for any person or persons . . . or attempt to ascertain the present, past, or future condition of any person or persons for gain or otherwise.

The religious fervor that would eventually make the city the "buckle on the Bible belt" was already in evidence. In 1885, when an itinerant Methodist preacher named Sam Jones passed through Nashville, he reportedly saved many souls. The daily newspaper, *The Banner*, wrote, "a religious movement is underway which promises to be the deepest and [most] far reaching ever witnessed in the city."

Among those who heard Jones, and whose life was forever changed, was Tom Ryman, a hard-living riverboat captain. He immediately ended the sale of liquor on his riverboats, which meant giving up a lucrative income stream. Particularly notorious drinkers were the crews who manned coal barges coming downriver from Kentucky. Tired and dirty when they reached Nashville, after unloading the coal, they boarded a steamboat for the return trip, and were prone to celebrate by consuming a lot of liquor. After Tom Ryman found religion in 1885, most of them probably switched their patronage to other steamboats.

The city housed 170 saloons, and Tom Ryman owned the largest. After hearing Sam Jones preach, Ryman determined to use the place to raise up the Lord. He changed its name to Sam Jones Hall, and henceforth, it was a place where not a drop of liquor crossed the threshold, a wonderful big space for revival meetings and itinerant preachers, as well as the place where the Temperance Society held its meetings. It was renamed for Tom Ryman after his death in 1904, and became the Mother Church of country music when WSM radio began broadcasting the Grand Ole Opry from the Ryman Auditorium in 1943.

Tom Ryman lived long enough to see his steamboat business start to decline because of competition from the railroads, and, in fact, it was a railroad that killed him. Horses pulling a wagon were spooked by a passing locomotive and rammed Tom Ryman's buggy. He eventually died from his injuries, and Sam Jones preached at his patron's funeral.

In 1906 about 35,000 Nashvillians identified as some form of Protestant, 6,000 as Catholics and three hundred as Jews. What community spirit and assistance to the poor that existed—and it wasn't much—usually originated in churches on both the white and black sides of the railroad tracks. The Nashville Colored Ladies Relief Society was formed in 1886 to help the neediest in the black community. Two prominent faith-based white groups were the Nashville Relief Society, which dispensed food, clothing, and coal to those families who could not afford them, and the Woman's Mission Home, which provided shelter for prostitutes, unwed mothers, and other "fallen women."

Tennessee Centennial Exposition, from May 1 to October 31, 1897. Print shows a bird's-eye view of the Exposition's grounds and buildings, published by the Henderson Lithographing Company, Cincinnati, December 7, 1896.

Much of the energy of churchgoing women was taken up by the temperance movement. It would be thirty years before the Prohibitionists had their way, but have it they would, with the eighteenth amendment to the Constitution, which took effect in 1920, and lasted until 1933. The amendment was the result of a 35-year struggle to achieve a "dry" nation, and the early roots of that movement were deep in places like Nashville's churches. The early temperance movements had an uphill battle against Nashville's 170 saloons, and the fondness of its citizens for the good life: rich meals augmented by good wine, the conviviality around a glass or two of whiskey.

Nevertheless, the Prohibitionists persisted, and by the end of the nineteenth century, the temperance movement was exercising a powerful influence on Nashville's politics. Churchgoers felt that they not only must be good, but should encourage good in others. One way was to help the needy and the poor. Another was to eliminate temptation in the form of demon rum. Historian Don Doyle described the emotions behind Nashville's temperance movement in his book *Nashville in the New South, 1890–1930*: "Drunkenness was seen as the root cause of so many other evils, its eradication seemed to promise deliverance to a radically improved moral order."

On the opposing side, the city had its fair share of men who made an excellent living from distilling whiskey, or brewing beer, and others who did quite well selling them. To match the popular rallies of the temperance crusade, they mounted their own, maintaining that the cause was being used by the Republican Party to regain the political influence it had lost in the state following the Civil War.

In 1887 an election was held to determine if the state constitution should be amended to prohibit the sale of alcohol. The run-up to the election was frenzied. The Protestant churches mounted large-scale rallies, and congregations were urged to pray. The anti-Prohibitionists sent kegs of beer to neighborhoods throughout the city, and the amendment was soundly defeated. Historians point out that the temperance movement marked the first time women began to organize themselves politically, and as such, it was the beginning of the struggle by women for the vote.

Issues such as Prohibition and segregation deeply divided the city, even as it grew and prospered. But Nashville finished the nineteenth century with a grand community spectacle, the Tennessee Centennial Exposition, featuring a life-size replica of the Parthenon to remind visitors that Nashville was, indeed, the Athens of the South. The Centennial Exposition served, among other things, as a point of pride for all the city's residents. It was built in West Side Park, renamed Centennial Park, and was visited by some 1.8 million people over the span of six months from May through October 1897.

The exposition's organizers were determined that it reflect a progressive, modern city, although alcohol, while available all over the city, would not be sold on the grounds. They strove hard to show Northern visitors to the exposition that the doctrine of separate-but-equal promoted a racial harmony that worked for both white and black people. The exposition had a Women's Department and a Negro Department, both of which featured speeches, special exhibits, and honorary days. A separate, striking "Negro Building" was constructed, which housed nearly three hundred exhibits, and had a restaurant serving black visitors to the exposition. Eight days of the six months were set aside as Negro Days, on which African Americans were given a reduced ticket price.

Both nature and technology were celebrated, along with history, art, and music. And there was an amusement park for youngsters. At exactly noon on May 1, 1897, President William McKinley inaugurated the Centennial Exposition by pressing a button in Washington, DC, which telegraphed an electrical impulse instantaneously to Nashville, setting off a cannon and an electric dynamo at the exposition. The president would grace Nashville with his actual presence in early July. The event was a resounding success, not only as an economic boon to the city, but for giving it invaluable national publicity. It was, perhaps, the first time Nashvillians proudly thought of themselves as residents of an "It" city.

Union Station, 20th-century photograph.

5 The City Spreads Out

The impetus given to development by the Centennial Exposition carried on into the new century. In 1900 the elegant Union Station, with its vaulting Romanesque Revival architecture, opened with a new train shed in an expanded railroad yard, replacing a dilapidated, second-rate depot, and emphasizing the importance of the city to rail travel for both passengers and freight in the Southeast. The new station's imposing stone structure was highlighted by a tower rising over 220 feet (67 m) and topped by a copper statue of Mercury, winged messenger of the gods. The waiting room was an ornate, domed space, rising 65 feet (20 m) into the air, which enclosed a large stone fireplace.

At the beginning of the twentieth century, with the market crash of 1893 receding into memory, commerce and business resumed their rightful place as Nashville's driving engines. The total amount of money that passed through local banks, their "clearings," quadrupled between 1900 and 1915. Insurance companies became an increasingly important component of Nashville's economy. A swarm of agents went into the field, selling financial protection from injury and death. When the Life and Accident Insurance Company opened in Nashville in 1903, its first paid health claim came from an elderly African American woman whose hand had become infected when she cut it on a washboard. All the company's executives came to the woman's rundown house to present her with a claims check for $2.25. Insurance companies became a pillar of the city's economy.

As more and more people moved out to the suburbs, and business expanded, Downtown land became increasingly valuable for

Real-estate advertisement from the *Nashville Tennessean*, 1926, which proclaims the arrival of a "Colored Sub-division."

its commercial value. People still came Downtown to shop, as they would for the next fifty years, even while moving en masse to live in the suburbs. Early in 1902, for instance, the last home on Downtown's Church Street was sold, and was demolished in order to build a department store.

In 1903 Nashville's first mall was opened in the heart of Downtown, an enclosed, block-long arcade with a glass roof, and more than fifty shops at both ground level and around the balcony. The Arcade connected Cherry and Summer Streets (later renamed Fifth and Fourth Avenues). Arcades were built in big cities around the world: Milan, Italy; Osaka, Japan; Paris, France; Quetzaltenango, Guatemala; and a host of others. Nashvillians were proud to have one of their own.

The opening of the Arcade was celebrated with great fanfare. The railroads offered discounted tickets for those riding to Nashville from the surrounding countryside to see it. A band was installed on the balcony, and played music throughout the day. As many as 50,000 people were reported to have passed through. The *Nashville American* reported that

On every hand were heard expressions of surprise and gratification at the completeness and variety of the stores. It has been the intention of the promoters of the Arcade to have the stores represent as many different lines as possible, and the result is that one can obtain anything from a shave to a piano at the Arcade.

The century's first decade saw two presidents visit the city. Theodore Roosevelt put up at the stately Maxwell House, and William Howard Taft was treated to a sumptuous banquet at the recently opened Hermitage Hotel. Two office buildings went up during those years, each twelve stories tall, towering over Downtown, and they were referred to as skyscrapers by the local citizenry. The second bank in the nation owned by an African American, the Freedman's Savings and Trust Company Bank, was opened. In *Face of Two Centuries*, John Egerton wrote,

Nashville had become a regional trade and manufacturing center—it produced a lion's share of the South's flour and corn

The Arcade, 20th-century photograph.

The Arcade, 21st-century photograph.

Hermitage Hotel, early 1900s, postcard.

meal, roasted most of its coffee, and supplied the region with more dry goods, shoes, groceries, hardware, lumber, and building supplies than any other city south of the Ohio River.

The first horseless carriages were already on Nashville's dusty streets as the new century opened. By 1908 some five hundred Nashvillians owned one. The number of automobiles would keep growing, and improving streets and roads would soon be high on the list of priorities of any local politician hoping to be elected. The move to the suburbs was greatly facilitated by the automobile, and soon a white Nashville resident walking on Downtown streets in the evenings was a rare sight, and those who did so were likely up to no good.

Downtown was still insalubrious, which did not add to its attractiveness. O. Henry, the noted journalist and short-story writer, described his 1909 arrival in Nashville:

A Few of Nashville's City Ordinances, 1909

It shall be unlawful for any person, firm or corporation to have, maintain or conduct any house, room, place, den or resort where opium is sold, to be consumed or smoked at said place, conduct or maintain any room, den, or resort, or where people assemble to smoke or consume opium in any manner or form; or to keep, conduct, maintain any room, house, place, den or resort for the purpose of prostitution, illegal commerce between the sexes, or sexual depravity, natural or unnatural . . .

Whoever shall, in this city, appear in any public place naked, or in a dress not belonging to his or her sex, or in an indecent or lewd dress, or shall make any indecent exposure of his or her person, or be guilty of any indecent or lewd act or behavior, or shall exhibit, sell of offer for sale, any obscene, vulgar, or libellous book, picture, painting, paper or publication of any character whatever that shall be adjudged vulgar, libellous or indecent, immoral or lewd play or other representation, shall be deemed guilty of a misdemeanor.

Any white male or female found living or cohabiting with, as man and wife, any negro, mulatto, or person of mixed blood descended from a negro, shall be deemed guilty of a misdemeanour and fined not less than twenty nor more than fifty dollars.

The washing of horses and vehicles on the streets shall be a nuisance, and the person so offending shall be subject to a fine of five dollars.

This 1907 editorial cartoon from the *Nashville Banner* depicts the city as a woman with a dark blemish on her cheek, and asks what can be done to remove it.

I stepped off the train at 8 P.M. Having searched the thesaurus in vain for adjectives, I must, as a substitution, hie me to comparison in the form of a recipe.

Take a London fog 30 parts; malaria 10 parts; gas leaks 20 parts; dewdrops gathered in a brick yard at sunrise, 25 parts; odor of honeysuckle 15 parts. Mix.

The mixture will give you an approximate conception of a Nashville drizzle. It is not so fragrant as a moth-ball nor as thick as pea-soup; but 'tis enough—'twill serve.

The city was a hub for train traffic and had both north-to-south and east-to-west lines. In July 1918, two passenger trains bore down on a single stretch of track; they were coming from, and going to, Memphis. One should have given way, but neither did, and they collided head-on, each going about 60 mph (100 kph), as they came around a bend called Dutchman's Curve on the western edge of Belle Meade. Inside the wooden cars, 121 people died and 157 were injured. Some 50,000 Nashvillians came in the next 24 hours to help search for injured and dead, or just to gawk at the passenger cars strewn across the rail bed. It remains the worst railroad accident in the United States' history.

It was an unusual year for the city in other ways. Between September and November of that year, at the same time as an end to the First World War was being negotiated and signed, the Spanish flu swept the South, and Nashville was hard hit, with one in every three people affected. At first, public officials denied that an epidemic was in progress, but in short order, schools, theaters, churches, and pool halls were closed. By February 1919, when the epidemic was definitively over, it had accounted for 579 deaths. People died in all parts of town, but a general belief persisted that the suburbs were healthier, because they had a more ample supply of fresh air.

The suburbs may, or may not, have offered any more protection against the Spanish flu than Black Bottom, but in general, the city's white middle- and upper-classes found the suburbs suited them and their idea of the good life. A house, with a yard and a car in the garage, a nearby church, and a steady job made up their world, and

Dutchman's Curve train collision, July 9, 1918, Henry C. Hill photograph.

they were pleased with it. Suburban residents were mostly content to leave the direction of the city in the hands of "old Nashville," those families who had run the city for more than a century and continued to do so. The driving force behind city planning was to create a friendly urban atmosphere for making money, and leave well enough alone. Sin, for instance, was allowed to thrive, but only Downtown, and what went on down by the river, stayed there.

The part of Downtown called the "Men's Quarter," around what is now Fourth Avenue North, housed gambling clubs, bars, pawn shops, lawyers' offices, barbershops, Turkish baths, and brothels. Women were not seen there. One of the most notorious watering holes was the Southern Turf, which featured liquor downstairs, gambling upstairs, and waiting women on the third floor. Word spread among men around the South that a wild time was to be had in Nashville, and the rumors were not exaggerations.

As the city's population fanned out, and the suburbs grew, Downtown shrunk to a place where only the poorest Nashvillians lived.

An exception were a handful of elegant, older houses belonging to families that stubbornly refused to move, or which were transformed into boarding houses. Generally, however, the only reason a family lived Downtown was because they could not afford another choice, and the places where they lived were far from elegant. Black Bottom or the Men's Quarter were not places to raise your family if you had another option. It would be another century before Downtown was seen, again, as a good place to live, rather than just a place to go to work or play.

Interior of the Southern Turf Saloon, before 1920.

Owen Boarding House, 1910.

Culturally, the city continued to grow: an opera house was constructed, and the nation's leading opera companies and symphonic orchestras included Nashville on their tours, as did drama companies from the big cities. The first Nashville symphony orchestra was formed in 1904. In 1906 Sarah Bernhardt packed the Ryman Auditorium. Motion pictures were just beginning to catch on, and in short order, Nashville had half a dozen theaters, each charging 5¢ admission. Horse racing was popular, and the city's baseball team won the Southern League a number of times.

But the old divisions didn't disappear, and a pair of issues—alcohol and race—continued to generate controversy. Prohibition and segregation affected people's lives in a variety of ways. As early as 1902, the Anti-Saloon League was vociferously supporting anti-liquor candidates for both national and local office. Chief among the group's targets in Nashville was the Southern Turf, which had to support numerous police raids despite hefty pay-offs. In 1909 the Tennessee State Legislature effectively made the state "dry," when a law was passed making it illegal to "sell or tipple any intoxicating liquors, including wine, ale, and beer, within four miles of any schoolhouse, public or private, where a school is kept, whether the school be in session or not." That same year, however, in keeping with the contradictory nature that has always characterized the local attitude towards alcohol and sin in general, Nashvillians elected an anti-Prohibitionist mayor, Hilary E. Howse, who reassured the moneyed owners of clubs like the Southern Turf by stating, "As for whisky, I am not a drinking man, but as long as I stay in a free country I will eat and drink as I please."

The new Prohibition law still allowed for the importation of liquor bought in other states for private use, and clubs in the Men's Quarter immediately installed lockers where each man could leave a bottle, presumably one bought in some other state. But first, a state-wide anti-saloon injunction in 1914, and then a complete ban on alcohol in 1917, three years before it became national law, tightened the screws on the nightspots of the Men's Quarter.

Even after the 21st amendment was repealed in the rest of the country, Tennessee stayed dry—on paper, at least. Alcohol sales, consumption, and abuse continued through all those years of legal abstinence. Nashville maintained its legal veneer of respectability, but the reality was something else. There was always somewhere to get a drink—as long as that drink was somewhere that served members of your race.

A prominent black dentist, J. B. Singleton, born in 1902, recalled Nashville in the first two decades of the twentieth century when he was interviewed in 1979:

> The indignities of segregation and discrimination applied to all blacks, regardless of education or position or income. We learned early where we were allowed to go—upstairs in theaters, downstairs on steamboats, in the back on streetcars, in the front on trains. Everything was segregated—schools and churches, restaurants and hotels, restrooms and drinking fountains.

A memorial to Nashville's suffragette leaders by Alan LeQuire, in Centennial Park.

Nashville would pass through many changes and two world wars in the century's first fifty years, but the division of races stayed the same. One early important change that did happen was when, in August 1920, Tennessee passed the 36th vote of the 36 necessary to ratify the 19th amendment to the Constitution granting women the right to vote. Nashville's suffragettes were influential enough in changing the political climate to have brought the question before the voters, and to have carried the state.

The Great Depression of 1929 hit the city hard, but less so than many other places. Hard times were slow to arrive, and as late as October 1930, it was business as usual. Then, in November, the wave of financial ruin washed over Nashville's banks, brokerage firms, insurance companies, and real estate dealers. By the end of the year, unemployment was at 25 percent.

The Depression also brought Franklin Delano Roosevelt's New Deal policies to put people back to work, and the work programs left lasting benefits for Nashville. Among the buildings constructed using federal funds in the 1930s were a new post office, a courthouse, strictly segregated housing projects for black and white Nashvillians, a new airport, and eight new schools, as well as $2.5 million spent on paving and expanding city streets.

While far from the big-city centers of culture and fashion, Nashvillians continued to think of their city as the "Athens of the South," an important Southern cultural hub. The Fugitive literary movement, which drew national attention, was founded at Vanderbilt by Robert Penn Warren, who was later to become the nation's first poet laureate. He was joined by poets Allen Tate and John Crowe Ransom. The Fugitives came together in the mid-1920s, and by 1930 they wielded tremendous influence on the writing and teaching of poetry, enshrining a formal style of meter, rhyme, and stanza.

Another closely aligned group was the Agrarians, and in 1930 they published a collection of essays called *I'll Take My Stand*, which included pieces by Tate, Ransom, and Warren. The Agrarians rejected the fast-paced industrialization of the North, and praised the way of life in the agrarian South. These movements exalted regional writing, and brought a new respect to the Southern canon of poetry and fiction, while remaining a club in which membership was restricted to white men. From a twenty-first-century perspective, the Agrarians appear conservative, slightly racist, and a bit Luddite, but they enthusiastically revived the idea of Southern writing and literature in the early 1930s.

The changes in literary fashion may not have attracted much attention outside the walls of academe, but in 1937, widespread public excitement greeted the opening of the Tennessee State Museum in the War Memorial Building, on Legislative Plaza, a block away from the State Capitol. The General Assembly finally had been convinced that the state's collection of art and artifacts had reached such proportions that it needed permanent housing, and they appropriated the funds.

The museum's new quarters in the War Memorial building were not ideal. The collection was exhibited in the building's lower level, and the space was small and poorly lit. Nevertheless, a couple of generations of Tennesseans trouped through, including myself—numerous times. What drew me back whenever I had a chance to go was a 3,500-year-old Egyptian mummy that was laid out in a glass case. This is what death looked like, and I never tired of regarding it.

In 1981 the museum was moved to much larger, and more brightly lit, quarters in the James K. Polk building on the other side of Legislative Plaza, which it shared with the Tennessee Performing Arts Center. In October 2018, it moved to its current location, a new building on Rosa Parks Boulevard, close by the Farmers' Market and the Bicentennial Mall.

The museum's opening in 1937 was only one indication of the optimism greeting the nation's recovery from the Depression. By 1940, the business volume of manufacturers, retailers, and wholesalers had surpassed pre-Depression levels, and for the first time ever, bank clearings were more than a billion dollars. By the Second World War, prosperity had returned, and war is never bad for business. Through all those fat and lean years, Nashville's African Americans were obliged to live as second-class citizens when dealing with white people.

Even so, an African American business community had grown up in North Nashville, reflecting the one on the white side of the tracks. Both death and life provided business impetus, and still do: everything from funerals and burials to haircuts and doctors was done in the black community by African Americans. North Nashville's black elite was, in part, as rigid in its social mores as the white elite, and just as skilled at feigning ignorance about things like gambling halls and brothels.

While white and black Nashvillians suffered alike during the Second World War, losing family members and friends, those young men who survived and came back faced hugely different lives and unequal opportunities. On the battlefields, black men had fought and died with white men, but in Nashville, they were supposed to accept being oppressed, divided, and segregated—to settle, at best, for separate but equal, and at worst, separate but unequal. They would always be served last and blamed first. It would soon become

Walter Swett and his son, Swett's Market, 1947.

apparent, however, that veterans returning to the South were no longer as willing to accept second-class citizenship.

Nashville came out of the war suffering from stagnation, according to some observers. It was a genteel, conservative city, resistant to progress, slow to acknowledge that it would have to modernize both its infrastructure and its attitudes if it was to compete effectively with other cities of its size. But thanks to its broad base of banking, insurance, manufacturing, music, and publishing, it quietly prospered.

6 A Change Is Gonna Come

Postwar Nashville was the subject of an article by Rufus Jarman in a national magazine, the *Saturday Evening Post*, on October 27, 1951. He observed that Nashvillians were generally suspicious of progress, and were very attached to the status quo:

> Therein lies Nashville's greatest weakness and its greatest charm. The true Nashvillian is more interested in living as his grandfather did than in having his city a model of civic progress. In many homes, life moves along with an old-fashioned ease that usually captivates people from the big cities to the north.

That staid, comfortable existence could not last. The winds of change were coming, but before they arrived, Nashville passed a placid decade in the 1950s. Business picked up, the suburbs were built out with spacious brick houses set on wide, sloping lawns, with two-car garages large enough to accommodate each year's increasingly longer models, and people had televisions to watch in the evenings. Alcohol was not served in public, and the city maintained a facade of absolute respectability. Anything deviating from the norm was suspicious and probably felonious. The suburbs continued to be where people chose to make their homes. In 1960, for the first time, the city of Nashville's population was smaller than that of Davidson County surrounding it.

People still came Downtown to shop, but by the end of the war, "respectable" people no longer lived Downtown. The boarding houses and staid, old single-family homes scattered throughout

Escalator at Harvey's, 1958.

Downtown were demolished and replaced with more commercial establishments. Still, Downtown had its attractions, including three large department stores, along with a handful of movie theaters, and lots of lunch counters and hamburger joints, all of them offering milkshakes and banana splits, where white people could sit to consume their food and drink, while black people were not welcome.

For a white kid during the 1950s, an exciting Saturday was a trip Downtown to ride the escalators at Harvey's Department Store, and drink a chocolate milkshake at the whites-only soda fountain there called the Monkey Bar, in a room featuring real monkeys in a huge cage. When Fred Harvey opened his department store in 1943, the escalators were the first in town. So too was the cage full of monkeys. By the time I was born, Harvey's was Nashville's largest store, eventually occupying the entire north side of Church Street between Fifth and Sixth Avenues. After riding the escalators as many times as a parent would allow, a Downtown Saturday afternoon was rounded out with a movie at one of Church Street's three large, air-conditioned movie theaters.

The Tennessee State Fair was open for a week in the fall, offering rides, games, freak shows, and agricultural exhibits. The midway crowds generated an energy and excitement that was not on offer during the rest of the year. Nashville didn't get its first skyscraper until 1957, when the Life and Casualty Insurance Company put up what was known as the Life & Casualty Tower (or L&C Tower). Its thirty floors, jutting out at an angle over Church Street and Fourth Avenue, made it the tallest building in the state when it was inaugurated. It was to stand for decades as the anchor of the skyline, a visible sign that Nashville had big-city aspirations.

Back when the L&C Tower was new, the most exciting live sports event of the year was the annual high school football championship, called the Clinic Bowl. It was played on Thanksgiving Day in crisp autumn air at the Vanderbilt University stadium, where men in long woolen overcoats gathered at halftime under the bleachers to sip discretely from flasks.

About the best sport a kid could hope to watch if it was spring or summer was minor-league baseball, a home game for the Nashville

Vols. Their stadium, Sulphur Dell, was the oldest still-active ball-park in the nation, built in 1870 beside the site of the original sulfur spring. High school football and minor league baseball were modest athletic events for a city that half a century later hosts professional football and hockey teams at the highest levels. Nissan Stadium is a huge 69,000-seat football stadium for the Tennessee Titans, a National Football League franchise; and the Bridgestone Arena, opened in 1996, holds more than 17,000 screaming hockey fans for the Nashville Predators' home games in the National Hockey League.

The summers are terribly hot in Nashville, the hills surrounding the city trapping an oppressive, humid heat, and in the 1950s, air conditioning was scarce. Kids took full advantage of swimming pools, spending whole days with their mothers at a poolside: for the not-so-fortunate, there were public pools, and for the children

State Fair, 1950.

Life & Casualty Tower, designed by Edwin Keeble. Completed in 1957.

of the well-to-do, every country club had a pool where kids spent entire days. The public Cascade Plunge was where I learned to swim, the place where I and many others took that first risk of putting our faces in the water, guided by a patient college student making money during the summer as a swimming instructor. Cascade Plunge was one of the neighborhood pools used exclusively by white people. Black Nashvillians had their own. Occasionally, during the not-infrequent polio epidemics that swept the city, all the pools would be closed.

Polio was a scourge, leaving youngsters crippled, or in iron lungs. Still, even when the Salk vaccine against polio became available, many parents were distrustful and reluctant to have their kids vaccinated. An early proponent of the vaccine was John J. Lentz, a physician who graduated from Vanderbilt Medical School in 1906, and devoted his whole career to public health in Nashville. This was, he often said, because he lost his sister to diphtheria and his father to lockjaw. Nashville's main public health clinic is named after him.

For a teenager during those years, the available pleasures were suburban in nature. The lucky ones were allowed to use the family car on the weekends. Those Friday and Saturday nights were filled by dances; a little illegal alcohol obtained any way possible; trips to the Hippodrome, a vast, old wooden roller-skating rink on West End Avenue; and increasingly, by rock and roll. Nashville's fundamentalist clergy grew evermore alarmed, warning of the evils to which rock and roll was leading the young, pointing at Elvis Presley's gyrating hips.

Cascade Plunge, August 1958.

Hippodrome Skating Rink, 1958.

Those worried pastors were right. Even in the city that was home to the Grand Ole Opry, rock and roll, with its roots deep in African American music, rapidly became the favorite music of the young. This shift in record sales was, perhaps, an early warning signal that the world around them was changing, but for many older Nashvillians, life unfolded during the 1950s in a placid and predictable manner.

Then the 1960s arrived.

The decade was less than two months old when the Nashville "sit-ins" began in February 1960, aimed at desegregating the city's lunch counters. Students from Fisk University and American Baptist College, both predominantly African American schools, decided to follow the recent example of students in Greensboro, North Carolina, and demand the right to be served at Downtown lunch counters. Black Nashvillians spent a lot of money in Downtown department

Sit-in, spring 1960.

stores, or the five-and-dime stores like Woolworth's or Kresge's, but they were not allowed to sit at the lunch counters in these same stores.

The students dedicated themselves to changing this by using nonviolent, civil disobedience. In Nashville, they were schooled in this Ghandian strategy by a local theologian and minister named James Lawson, who began holding workshops on nonviolent tactics in the fall of 1959. In Nashville, as in so many Southern cities, it was the African American clergy who led the way towards integration, men like James Lawson, and his friend Kelly Miller Smith, who was the pastor of Nashville's largest and most important black congregation, the First Baptist Church.

Students from Lawson's workshops would come to one of Downtown's segregated lunch counters, sit down, and wait to be served. The manager would come out and tell them that he only served white people. The students would continue to sit, waiting and waiting. The lunch counter would be closed. Invariably, young whites would arrive, and gather behind where the students were sitting to spit on them, or burn them with cigarettes, or punch them, knocking them off their stools. Lawson had taught them how to respond, and they got up off the floor and sat back down, ready to be punched again. They endlessly turned the other cheek; they offered neither resistance nor violence.

The Nashville lunch counter sit-ins quickly began to generate mass arrests—of the protestors. At first, the older, more conservative black community feared retaliation and reprisal by whites, but local religious leaders like Kelly Miller Smith convinced the community-at-large to institute a boycott of Downtown businesses in March 1960. The city's buses and businesses were deserted. People made do by carpooling, and gave up the pleasure of Easter shopping Downtown. A high percentage of the black community observed the boycott, and the effect on Downtown's businesses was profound. "Millions of dollars are being lost by the city of Nashville over a 25-cent hamburger," commented Vivian Henderson, a Fisk economics professor.

It was a life-changing experience for many people, both black and white, to witness the students' nonviolence in their efforts to right the long-lasting wrongs they had suffered for so many years.

Ira Sandperl and Rev. James Lawson lead discussion at the annual Southern Christian Leadership Conference staff workshop, Penn Center, Frogmore, South Carolina, 1966. Photograph by Bob Fitch.

Martin Luther King, Jr. with Kelly Miller Smith before speaking at Fisk University in April 1960.

In April, Martin Luther King, Jr. visited Fisk to lend his support: "I came to Nashville not to bring inspiration, but to gain inspiration from the great movement that has taken place in this community."

Tensions reached their highest level in April with the bombing of the home belonging to Z. Alexander Looby, the lead attorney for the arrested student protestors. The bomb blast blew the front off of his house and broke windows up and down the block. The next day, thousands of people marched silently from North Nashville to the courthouse. The mayor, Ben West, was there to receive them. Diane Nash, one of the student leaders, asked the mayor if he personally thought the lunch counters should serve everyone regardless of race. Yes, he answered, noting later that he had answered her from a moral point of view. The mayor's support made the difference, and, shortly thereafter, in May 1960, desegregation took effect in Downtown eateries.

The sit-ins spread to the three Downtown movie theaters, where segregation restricted African Americans to "colored" sections in the balconies. They were supposed to buy their tickets at a side entrance, and climb a flight of stairs to the balcony, never mixing with white patrons. The students organized "stand-ins." I watched them line up at the white person's ticket window of the Paramount Theater up Church Street from my family's bookstore. One by one, they approached the window and asked for a ticket. The ticket-seller would refuse with a shake of his head, and often a mean-looking guy would step up from the knot of angry white men standing by, and punch the students in their jaws, or shove them to their knees. The young person would get up off the sidewalk, go to the back of the line, and repeat the procedure, until the police came and broke up the stand-in by arresting the students. That was a long time ago, and I have seen a lot of amazing things since then, but nothing ever affected me more deeply, or made me think harder.

It was one thing to desegregate the buying-and-selling process—lunches and movie tickets—but quite another to allow black and white boys and girls to mingle in bathing suits, so much flesh exposed, sharing the same water. At that time, the city had 22

Students march after the bombing at Z. Alexander Looby's home, 1960.

Diane Nash and Mayor Ben West on the courthouse steps.

public pools, and seven of them were designated for black people. Nashvillians of all races had to escape the heat somehow, but they had to do it with their own race.

One July 18, 1961, two young black Nashvillians were bored, hot, and in-between protests. They had participated in the early sit-ins, and with nothing better to do, they decided to go swimming—not at the local pool for African Americans, but at the public pool in Centennial Park, which was for whites only. Kwame Lillard and Matthew Walker were turned away when they got there, but the authorities took the incident as a warning that the city's pools were going to be the next targets for mass protests. Two days after the pair of black men were turned away from the Centennial pool, the Parks Board closed all of Nashville's pools in a pre-emptive strike.

None reopened for over two years, and the Centennial Park pool was filled in and never reopened. "We got criticism from both black and white, since no one could swim," Lillard told an interviewer many years later. "But we never imagined the Parks Board would do such a thing. We thought surely, surely, they wouldn't drain the pools for two little black boys."

Local media played a large role in changing race relations. The last half of the twentieth century was a golden time for both newspapers and radio stations. In those pre-Internet decades, newspapers, radio, and television were the go-to sources of community news and information. Radio was a powerful force in those days. If a weather disaster was coming—a tornado or a blizzard—Nashvillians did not turn on the TV, or have a cell phone to go to for updates, they turned on the radio. The music these stations played was the principal determinant of popular culture, their broadcasts reaching millions across the South.

Nashville had two powerhouse broadcasters, WSM-AM and WLAC-AM, both of which reached listeners across the Southeast, and both of which had been broadcasting since the 1920s. Clear channel WSM had sent the Opry out across the airwaves since 1925, reaching young people living all across the Southeast who saved their money for a guitar, and dreamed of running away to Nashville and becoming

Nashville loved Elvis's *Loving You* in 1957.

Students block traffic on Church St., spring 1960.

stars. WSM grew into the most important disseminator of country music in the world. Today, the Opry on WSM is the world's longest-running live radio broadcast.

WLAC, on the other hand, made a big programming decision in the late 1950s and took to broadcasting rhythm and blues at night with a group of disc jockeys who were white, but sounded black, and had a keen appreciation for African American music. The best known was John Richbourg, whose late night program as John R. had a dedicated young audience on both sides of the tracks. The signal could be tuned in from Canada to Jamaica, spreading the gospel of rhythm and blues. In addition, a black-owned radio station, WVOL, came on Nashville's airwaves full time in 1960. Rock and roll crossed racial lines to generate joy among the young. Suddenly, the Devil's music was everywhere. Kids walked around with transistor radios and earbuds, and bought lots of 45-rpm records. White people were embracing black people's music, and opening up a whole new market.

Radio was not the only place Nashvillians went for their news. The last half of the twentieth century was a time of glory, and large profit margins, for Nashville's newspapers. The morning paper, the *Nashville Tennessean*, began publication in 1907, but claimed to be a direct descendant of the *Nashville Whig*, first published in 1812. The *Tennessean*'s competitor, the *Nashville Banner,* came out in the after-noons. *The Banner* was staunchly Republican, while the *Tennessean* was reliably Democratic, and there was a fierce competition for news between them.

In the 1970s and '80s, *The Tennessean* was presided over by editor-in-chief John Seigenthaler, who had also served as an aide to Attorney General Robert Kennedy during the early 1960s. Seigen-thaler was a Nashvillian from a working-class, Roman Catholic family, who had started as a reporter at the *Tennessean* in the 1950s, and worked his way up. He was generally deeply admired by the report-ers who worked for him, and he deftly managed a newsroom full of people who would one day be best-selling authors, among them David Halberstam and Tom Wicker. Al Gore, Jr., destined to be Bill Clinton's vice president for eight years and to have lost the 2000

John Seigenthaler at the Profile in Courage Awards ceremony at the John F. Kennedy Library in Boston, May 2003.

presidential election to George W. Bush by a contested recount, worked for Seigenthaler as a reporter from 1971 to 1974.

The Tennessean was not averse to funding long-term investigative projects. One of its reporters spent a year infiltrating the Ku Klux Klan. Another reporter, Frank Sutherland (later to follow Seigenthaler as editor-in-chief), a few years earlier, went under-cover as a patient for a month in the state mental institution, across the highway from Nashville's airport. Sutherland's award-winning eleven-part series, published in January 1974, opened,

> Central State Hospital is a warehouse for the storage of people — an unaccredited and unclean hospital with over half its doctors unlicensed to practice in Tennessee.
>
> I know. I just spent 31 days there.

In 1972 the city's two newspapers had been bought from their Nashville owners by the Gannett Company, which currently owns nearly 75 newspapers across the u.s., and a long process of corpo-ratization began. *The Banner* was shut down, making Nashville a

Stephen Gaskin during the Haight Street Fair at Golden Gate Park, San Francisco, on May 24, 1969.

one-newspaper, uncompetitive town, and the corporate version of *The Tennessean* did not have a lot of local news, nor much of a budget for long, investigative pieces. The corporation moved reporters and editors around, and eventually, few native Nashvillians were left on the staff as reporters or editors. This was reflected in the reportage (or lack thereof) of local stories. Local coverage was mostly redirected to entertainment and pop culture.

But that was later. Both newspapers thrived during the 1960s, and slowly but surely, the counterculture infiltrated the city, brought by people arriving from elsewhere: long-haired, non-churchgoing young people, worried about the military draft, and against the war in Vietnam. A coffeehouse called The Tulip Is Black opened in the mid-1960s, as did a couple of vegetarian restaurants, and a "head" shop selling marijuana paraphernalia.

In 1971 Nashville earned a place on the national hippie map thanks to Stephen Gaskin, a former u.s. Marine and English professor at California's San Francisco State College. Gaskin was also a psychedelic proselytizer, and every Monday night at the Family Dog auditorium in San Francisco, he gave a sermon on the benefits of communally ingesting mind-altering drugs, and the joys of living the hippie life. His exhortations to listen to the lessons of lysergic acid diethylamide (LSD) attracted weekly crowds of over a thousand.

In 1971 Gaskin left the West Coast with a caravan of some sixty vehicles that kept heading east until it reached Summertown, Tennessee, an hour south of Nashville. Some three hundred people accompanied him, and they purchased about 1,700 acres (700 ha) of farmland, establishing a vegetarian, pacifist, hippie community, much to the initial astonishment and dismay of Summertown's residents. However, all those new folks added to the revenue base, and eventually the small town grew to accept the presence of the communards who named their settlement The Farm.

The Farm grew steadily during the 1970s, reaching a peak of about 1,600 residents. Nashville was the closest city, and Farm members often went there to shop. Many of them did not stay at the Farm, becoming discouraged when they found that they had to work, and that all their money would be turned over to the communal treasury. Eventually, the Farm contributed to the city a goodly number of bright, young people who had grown disillusioned and decided to give Nashville a try.

When Stephen Gaskin was arrested in 1974 for growing marijuana, he did his jail time in Nashville. He could have pled guilty and avoided incarceration, but he chose to plead innocent, declaring that he grew weed for religious purposes and was not committing a crime. He was convicted and served a year. When he was released he was stripped of his voting rights, because he was a convicted felon. He challenged that law and won, restoring voting rights to hundreds of thousands of convicted felons. Gaskin died in 2014, but the Farm is still operational, thanks mostly to Ina May Gaskin, his widow, who is one of the world's foremost experts on midwifery. Aspiring and practicing midwives come from all over the world to train at Summertown.

These days, a young man—or woman for that matter—with long hair, tattoos, and piercings doesn't draw a second glance in Nashville's streets, but it was years after hippies were a common sight across much of the rest of the country when Nashvillians accepted that the 1950s were definitely gone, and they were not coming back. For instance, in 1961, a traveling appliance salesman from Florida, Robert Baldwin, opened a restaurant called Pancake Pantry in the Hillsboro Village neighborhood. The area is within walking distance of Vanderbilt University, and at that time, next to Downtown, the Village was Nashville's most popular place to shop.

The restaurant offered a standard array of dishes, but featured 27 different kinds of pancake on the menu. They were all made from Baldwin's exclusive buttermilk batter, and the place quickly became popular. In 1963 Baldwin reluctantly acquiesced to the citywide integration of restaurants, but until the mid-1970s, he steadfastly refused to serve any male with long hair. His policy generated a years-long boycott of Pancake Pantry by the more progressive elements of the city. By the time Baldwin's son took over in 1988, his father had changed his mind, and regardless of hair length, skin color, or any other distinguishing factor, anyone who wanted to eat there could do so. People still can, if they don't mind waiting in line for a seat, because it remains a popular place.

Nashville politicians, like those in the rest of the country, were occasionally prone to doing rather unsavory things. Political corruption was nothing new in Nashville, but a particularly embarrassing public scandal erupted around Bill Boner, a former congressman, who was elected mayor in 1987. In 1990 he appeared on the nationally broadcast *Phil Donohue Show* with an exuberant blonde, and announced that he was engaged to her, lauding the sexual intensity of his fiancée, although he was not yet divorced from his third wife. He had a slick, unctuous demeanor, an unfortunate last name, and was a laughingstock by the end of his first term. To no one's surprise, he did not run for a second. The man who won the 1992 election was cut from a different cloth. Phil Bredesen was a wealthy, well-educated man who led Nashville towards Big-Citydom with a firm hand, and would go on to be the Governor of Tennessee.

In 2018 Nashvillians had cause to remember the Boner years, as another mayor's sexual escapades again exposed the city to national ridicule. This time the miscreant was a woman. A popular and progressive first-term mayor—Nashville's first woman in the office—admitted to having had a torrid two-year affair behind her husband's back, with the chief of her security detail, a 31-year veteran of the Nashville police force. Worse, Mayor Megan Barry had paid with public funds for trips the two of them took. She resigned, and eventually pled guilty to felony theft, agreeing to repay $11,000 in exchange for no jail time and three years' probation.

Even while Bill Boner was making a fool of himself on national television, events were occurring that heralded the start of a more cosmopolitan Nashville. In 1987 the new international airport terminal was inaugurated, expanding the city's ability to handle flights; there were more and more people traveling to Nashville, and airport traffic was increasing. In 1996 regular flights between Nashville and London were inaugurated, and in that same year, the city opened the Bicentennial Mall, signaling the beginning of an intention to reclaim and develop the sketchier, more problematic Downtown

Ex-mayor Megan Barry, in office 2015–18.

Gaylord Opryland Resort and Convention Center.

neighborhoods, which had been ignored in favor of the suburbs for so many decades.

Many of the new visitors were coming to Opryland USA. In the early 1970s it had become obvious to the executives at radio station WSM, and its parent company the National Life and Accident Insurance Company, that the Grand Ole Opry had outgrown the Ryman Auditorium. A $40 million entertainment complex called Opryland USA was built, with a new auditorium for the Opry and an amusement park.

Until 1977 the city had little to offer in terms of a draw for conventions and congresses. That changed with the opening of the Opryland Hotel on the amusement park grounds. Initially, it had 580 guest rooms. As the years went on, it not only added rooms, but a conservatory with more than 10,000 plants and an indoor cascade, three-and-a-half stories high. The amusement park has since been replaced with a shopping mall, and the hotel houses fifteen restaurants. In 2018 the Opryland Hotel had more than 2,800 rooms and was one of the thirty largest hotels in the world. Already by the late 1980s, it was attracting more than 2.5 million visitors a year. Nashville was beginning to believe it had open-ended tourism potential, and it would not be long before the movers and shakers decided that Lower Broad was the next place to exploit it.

The city's leaders came to the view that Nashville was equal to the task of becoming one of the nation's great cities—not just a prosperous, self-satisfied, second-tier destination, but an "It city," as the *New York Times* was eventually to dub it. The new century would see the birth of a new Nashville, a city so transformed from its earlier self that there was no going back. Nashville greeted the twenty-first century committed to growth and change, and it would not be long in coming.

7 A New Nashville

For many years, the city's population was virtually entirely native-born. The number of foreigners in residence was minuscule. But in the 1970s, that began to change, and by 1980, some 10,000 foreign-born people were living in Nashville. Many were Mexicans, but others were from more exotic locales. The last two decades of the twentieth century saw a substantial influx of people from all corners of the globe.

Nashville was on a list of cities where the government sent refugees, and a substantial number of Vietnamese were resettled in Nashville after the war ended in 1975. By 1990 it was tagged as one of a small number of "gateway" cities, a place where immigrants could settle while they integrated into North American society. It wasn't long before people turned up who were fleeing from wars and brutal violence in places that many Nashvillians had not even heard of—refugees from terror and killing in places like Somalia, El Salvador, and Kurdistan. Many of these new residents talked up Nashville to relatives in other parts of the country.

At first, Nashvillians generally ignored the foreigners among them, other than to hire the women as domestic workers, and the men for lawn maintenance, or construction. A small mosque was inaugurated, and a number of evangelical churches holding services in Spanish opened in strip malls. A Buddhist temple was dedicated. The inner city's Catholic churches saw a jump in the numbers of people attending Mass. Slowly but surely, entrepreneurs among the newly arrived opened businesses that served the needs of their compatriots.

Plaza Mariachi Music City.

Between 1990 and 2018, the city's Hispanic population grew thirteenfold, one of the fastest growths in the nation, according to *The Economist*. By 2000, it was the third-fastest-growing Latino population in any U.S. city. Between 1994 and 2004, the city's public schools experienced a 1,133 percent growth in Hispanic students. By 2018, 10 percent of the city was Latino, the third largest ethnic population after European American and African American. A 2008 study concluded that 40 percent of the city's immigrants were from Mexico.

Why the rapid growth? The reasons the newcomers gave were various, but they sounded a lot like the reasons the new white-yuppie arrivals would give to the same question a decade later: it was a "nice" city, not too expensive, a good place to bring up kids, and the job market was good.

In addition, a certain sympathy for the South's macho concept of masculinity resonated with many men from rural parts of Mexico and Central America. They had no trouble understanding why a Nashville native might choose to own and drive a big pick-up truck, even if he never used it to haul anything; or why a man might choose to keep a rifle on a gun rack in that pick-up, and a 9-mm pistol in its

The Islamic Center of Nashville.

glove compartment; or why he might consider it stylish to wear pressed jeans with cowboy boots and a Stetson hat when he went out to dance and drink on a Saturday night. Other, more meaningful similarities existed. Mexicans and Latinos were religious, family-oriented people, not unlike their Nashville counterparts.

Regardless of what they might have had in common with the immigrants, many Nashvillians were dismayed by the growth of Mexican American Nashville. It took some adjustment, as was made clear to me on a personal level one midday while I was sitting in La Hacienda, the city's first and best taqueria on Nolensville Road. I was finishing a plate of tongue tacos, and idly gazing out the broad window into the parking lot, when I saw a woman driving a pick-up truck turn in and run directly into the rear end of my parked Volkswagen van.

She put the truck in reverse and turned around, preparing to pull out of the parking lot when I ran up to the driver's side window, yelling and waving my arms. She looked out her window, inquiringly, as if she couldn't imagine what I was doing there. "Hey," I hollered, "look at my van; you broke my taillight." Then I noticed her hands were trembling on the steering wheel, and tears were leaking out of her eyes. I repeated myself in Spanish. She told me, between sobs, that she had just borrowed her brother's pick-up to come get food; she was just visiting; she didn't have a driver's license—all the while interjecting her apologies, how sorry she was. She said that if the police came, she could be deported, and begged me just to let it go. I did, but I was $100 out of pocket to get that taillight fixed.

This was just the kind of situation that generated a decision in 2004 to issue "driving certificates" to people living in Tennessee who were illegally in the country, but would be driving anyway. With little public transportation, life in Nashville pretty much required a car, and it was the first thing most illegals bought. The certificates would be issued after people were tested on their driving skills, just like a

Cowboy hats for sale.

regular license, but would state prominently that it was not to serve as valid identification.

By 2005, some 21,000 had been issued, and it was rumored that people were coming from other states to obtain them, because despite the ban on using them for identification, they served that purpose quite well. In 2006 the program was abandoned. Because Tennessee had been the first to deal with drivers who were undocumented, the program's termination received some national press.

It was nothing, however, compared to what erupted when a special election was called in January 2009 to consider an addition to the city charter making English the official language in Nashville. All business with the city's government would have to be conducted in English. Backers maintained this would encourage immigrants to learn English, and reduce public spending for translators. The mayor and governor opposed it, as did the Chamber of Commerce. The vote was covered by the *New York Times*, all the large Latin American papers, and the wire services. The measure was rejected

The Gulch.

by 57 percent of the voters. Post-election analysis by the *Nashville Business Journal* showed that almost all the funding to promote the measure came from an anti-immigrant group, ProEnglish, based in Michigan.

The fears of the xenophobes turned out to be partially true. A flood tide of immigrants did eventually wash into Nashville, except that they were not from other countries, but from other parts of the United States, and they were young white people with disposable incomes. The city experienced remarkable growth following the economic crisis of 2008. By 2018, it had the lowest unemployment of any U.S. metropolitan area with more than a million residents. Many of the jobs were low-wage ones in the service sector, but many others were white-collar jobs.

The city these newcomers found was no longer a staid, old-money redoubt. By 2018 the LGBT Chamber of Commerce had some 325 members, representing all kinds of commercial activities. In early 2019 Nashville became the first Southern city to include specifically LGBT businesses as a category to be considered for municipal procurement orders. That was a long way from the days when the newspaper printed the names of those men soliciting sex from other men.

Nashville was showing itself willing to discard old barriers, and open itself to the new century. For many, a chance to move there was a welcome opportunity. In 2018 the New York financial firm Alliance-Bernstein announced it would relocate its corporate headquarters to Nashville, bringing more than a thousand jobs. This was followed by Amazon's decision to build its new $230 million Eastern Retail Operations Center in the Gulch, an upmarket Downtown neighborhood. It is expected to employ some 5,000 people, including numerous white-collar positions. These kinds of corporate-level jobs were filled by just the kind of middle-of-the-road, hardworking people who have characterized the city since its beginnings. Many of those hundred people a day who are moving to Nashville will find work, and fit right in. The downside is that Amazon's presence is expected to boost already-high real estate prices in the Gulch, and the city around it.

While the changing face of Nashville may be driven by new arrivals, the question of what kind of city it will be revolves around many of the same issues as always. Inclusion of all Nashvillians in enjoying the fruits of the city is still remote, even as Nashville becomes unrecognizable from what it was only a quarter century ago. As the city transforms, longtime, lower-income residents are forced out. For instance, census figures showed that until 2011, the Edgehill neighborhood on the southern edge of the city center was two-thirds African American, but between 2012 and 2016—in just four years—that balance had changed to about 50 percent black and 50 percent white.

A local television station took a poll on the first day of 2019, asking over a thousand Nashvillians if they would like the city's growth to slow. Eighty-three percent said they would. And growth will assuredly eventually diminish, but it does not appear likely to happen any time soon. When it does, and the rapid pace of transformation slows, it remains to be seen what sort of city has taken the place of the one that has disappeared.

THE CITY TODAY

Country Music Hall of Fame.

Music City, USA

Nashville's moniker of "Music City" is widely believed to be down to the city being the worldwide headquarters of the country music industry. Not so. It is, indeed, the worldwide headquarters, but that's not how it got its nickname. Legend has it that when Queen Victoria heard the Fisk Jubilee Singers during their 1873 tour to raise money for their university, she said admiringly that they must hail from "Music City." That tour raised enough money to save Fisk from financial collapse, and was the first time that music served such an important economic role in Nashville.

Regardless of who first applied the title, it's an apt one. In 2017 the music industry supported more than 56,000 jobs in the Nashville area and had a $10 billion economic impact on the region, according to Randy Boyd, commissioner of the Tennessee Department of Economic and Community Development. There are record companies, publishing firms, recording studios, and the people who service them: publicity agents, digital workers, and scores of other ancillary music industry businesses.

Musicians and songwriters are all over town, some in mansions and others renting a single furnished room. Most are somewhere in-between—working musicians who are paying off a mortgage and raising a family, with music at the center of work and play. Many a dinner party at someone's house will end with guests of all ages sitting around after supper playing music.

In addition to the musicians, there are the legions of songwriters who live in Nashville, supplying stars and their studio musicians with songs to record. The city is known as a place favorable to

Minnie Pearl and Mayor Ben West onstage at the Opry, *c.* 1950s.

"co-writing," and on any given day, pairs of hopeful songwriters are elaborating melodies, noodling on guitars and pianos, and searching for just the right lyrics. One hit song is enough to catapult a song-writer into a higher income bracket, and guarantee that any future work will at least draw a listen.

Country music itself originally came down from the mountains, the Appalachians: a proletarian, people's music, with roots in Ireland and England; a poor white person's music that didn't require more than vocal cords and a guitar, a banjo, or a fiddle. There are lots of narratives of hard times, giving naked voice to suffering a-plenty, mixed with a touch of spirituals, and gospel.

Harlan Howard, a singer-songwriter, producer, and Country Music Hall of Fame inductee, famously said that a country song consisted of "three chords and the truth." The music lent itself well to a certain post-Second World War genre of fast living for country singers like Hank Williams and Waylon Jennings. Another of their number, Johnny Cash, pulled himself together, gave up his amphetamine habit, and launched a national prime-time television show, which aired from 1969 to 1971, featuring some of the best talent of his day. *The Johnny Cash Show* was taped weekly at the Ryman Auditorium, and the first broadcast featured Joni Mitchell and Bob Dylan, performing with Cash. Later shows presented a wide range of performers from Stevie Wonder to Willy Nelson to Pete Seeger.

Country music began to shed its label as "redneck, hillbilly music" and expand its reach and appeal to a wider audience, including the 1960s generation. While country music stars were virtually all white, there were some notable crossovers—singers such as Charley Pride, or the great Ray Charles, whose country album issued

Johnny Cash performing at the Opry, late 1950s.

American music group the Prisonaires perform for fellow inmates in the yard of Tennessee State Prison, Nashville, September 1953.

in 1962, *Modern Sounds in Country and Western Music,* was such an immediate hit that the record label put out a "Volume Two" of the same title. A handful of African American country songwriters like Dobie Gray pitched their work to the studios. In 2012 Darius Rucker became the first African American to be invited to join the Grand Ole Opry since Charley Pride in 1993.

Since the 1960s, Nashville also has been home to a different kind of singer-songwriter. These people are more than singers or songwriters—they are poets, often using the same country music chords and rhythms to transmit something entirely different from the standard fare. Their music is an earthy, soulful mixture of country and folk music with lyrics that speak poetically of human experience. A host of terrific singer-songwriters in this genre have made Nashville their home—people like Townes Van Zandt, Guy Clark, Emmylou Harris, Nanci Griffith, Steve Earle, Rodney Crowell, John Prine, Tom House, and David Olney. Now they're dead, or in their sixties and seventies, but another generation of singer-songwriters in Nashville are right behind them, picking up where they left off. People like Paul Burch, Paul Thorn, Rhiannon Giddens, and many others carry on the tradition of using country music's instruments and rhythms to make musical poetry.

North Nashville, during the 1960s and '70s, had its own live music and its own places to hear it, clubs with names like the Black Diamond, the Club Baron, Club Stealaway, Del Morocco, and Brown's Dinner Club. The people who passed through to play in these places were top-flight musicians, including Little Richard, Ray Charles, Duke Ellington, and Count Basie. From 1962 to 1963, a young Jimi Hendrix gigged at numerous North Nashville clubs, before taking a job as Little Richard's guitar player on the midnight television program *Night Train*. Produced by WLAC, the syndicated program aired on Saturday nights and was hosted by a WVOL executive, Noble Blackwell. Hendrix also played at the New Era club on Charlotte Avenue, the same venue where Etta James recorded a live album.

One of the first rhythm and blues groups in the South was made up of five African American inmates at the state prison in Nashville, who were doing time for some heavy crimes like rape and murder. They called themselves the Prisonaires, and their 1953 doo-wop release "Just Walkin' in the Rain" was a big hit for Sun Records, the Memphis record label that would later record the likes of Elvis Presley and Jerry Lee Lewis.

For many years, virtually the only live music club for white folks Downtown, except for the strip clubs in Printer's Alley, was the Station Inn. An inconspicuous, low building, serving only beer and the most basic snacks, it opened in 1974; over the years, the finest bluegrass musicians in the world have graced its small stage. As the

Ryman was the mother church of country music, so the Station Inn was, and is, the mother church of bluegrass music, the wonderful stringed offshoot of country, which hearkens back to early mountain music.

An impressive number of songwriters and singers have had their careers launched or boosted by playing at The Bluebird Cafe, a small ninety-seat club in a Green Hills neighborhood strip mall. It was opened in 1982 by Amy Kurland. A long list of performers, including Taylor Swift, Garth Brooks, Patty Loveless, Faith Hill, and Pam Tillis, played there early in their careers. In 2008 the Nashville Songwriters Association International acquired the club, and now seating there has to be reserved months ahead of time.

While country music's big names may not perform often in their hometown, every year an event called the Country Music Association (CMA) Music Fest provides fans an opportunity to approach aspiring and established country stars. In addition to constant performances over the course of three days, the performers station themselves in booths where fans can get autographs.

As Nashville has grown, so have the opportunities to hear live music of all kinds. Rock and roll, rap, pop, indie rock, hip-hop, techno, Latin, and folk all have found audiences, and places to be

Bluegrass band playing at the Station Inn.

Craig Wiseman and special guest Taylor Swift perform onstage at The Bluebird Cafe on March 31, 2018.

heard. The Station Inn is no longer a white person's sole Downtown music venue, although bluegrass fans from around the world still consider it Nashville's most outstanding asset. The young residents of the Gulch high-rises have a good deal of disposable income, and they have generated a lively city-center club scene.

While country certainly rules the Nashville roost, other kinds of music have taken solid root. There's a jazz club, and all the salsa and Latin music anyone might want. In keeping with Nashville's ability to please the highbrow and the lowbrow, the Blair School of Music, affiliated with Vanderbilt University, hosts classical and chamber music concerts by exceptional musicians. The Nashville Symphony Orchestra was founded in 1946, and its current home, the $123 million Schermerhorn Symphony Center, was opened in 2006 and touts itself as having some of the best acoustics in the world.

To accommodate the lowbrows, there are still a few holdovers from the old Nashville school of honky-tonks. Brown's Diner, a converted trolley car that holds Nashville's oldest license to serve beer, demonstrates that it is still possible to combine a welcoming atmosphere and a honky-tonk vibe. Brown's, at the southern edge of Hillsboro Village, offers a reasonably priced menu of fried foods,

Lenny Kravitz performing on the LP Field stage in downtown Nashville during CMA Fest 2013.

and the only alcohol is Budweiser beer. "You can have any beer you want on draft," the bartender says, "as long as it's Bud."

There's a long, low diner ceiling over the bar in front, and at one end is a minuscule space, which accommodates five musicians, tops. The dining room is in the back, and the whole place looks like it was condemned yesterday. Even though smoking is no longer allowed inside Brown's, the air here still smells a bit like tobacco. The music is rock and roll, or country, or Americana, and the musicians are always better than competent.

A few other down-home bars have managed, so far, to avoid being crushed by development. The Springwater Supper Club and Lounge, across from the west side of Centennial Park, looks like one strong wind might do the deed, but it has already held up for over a century. The name is the fanciest thing about it. Renamed the Springwater in 1978, a tavern in this same place is said to have served liquid refreshment to visitors during the Centennial Exposition in 1897. It was a speakeasy during Prohibition, and the infamous boot-legger Al Capone is reputed to have enjoyed gambling there. Currently, it is a prime venue for indie- and punk-rock bands.

Then there is Bobby's out on Charlotte Pike, and Carol Ann's on Murfreesboro Road, both places where the beer is cold, and some excellent pickers are often getting together to spend an evening playing and singing. These are good places to hear young musicians honing their skills before going on to greater things and bigger venues.

Many local musicians, both from Vanderbilt's Blair School of Music and the recording studios, donate their time to the W. O. Smith Community Music School. The school was named after the man who had the idea to create it. William Oscar Smith was a stand-up bass player from Philadelphia with a doctorate in education. He lived in Nashville and taught music at Tennessee State University until he retired. Before settling in Nashville, he had played with jazz legends such as Charlie Parker, Bessie Smith, and the great trumpet player Dizzy Gillespie. "Of all the musicians I've had the pleasure of associating with, I can say that Oscar Smith was among the most gifted," said Gillespie, in his foreword to Smith's autobiography, *Sideman*. "His timing and resolution were almost perfect. He helped me discover my own sense of harmony and rhythm."

For many years, Smith had imagined a school that offered music lessons to low-income children. He was an active and subtle

Music lesson at W. O. Smith School.

integrationist, who strongly believed that music was a great glue for binding people together. He played cello for nearly twenty years with the Nashville Symphony Orchestra, and backed various jazz musicians. In the 1970s, he founded the Wednesday Night Club, which brought together a dozen men on a monthly basis—six white, six black—to sit around, drink, and talk. One of the men was the Dean of Music at Blair, and another was the editor-in-chief of *The Tennessean.* The club members encouraged W. O. when he talked about his idea for a music school, and it began to come together.

The school opened in 1984 in a rented house in the Edgehill neighborhood. In 2008 it moved to new quarters in an inner-city space in the same neighborhood, formerly occupied by a tire warehouse and retail store. It was completely redesigned by local architects. Young people from low-income families pay 50¢ a lesson, and are taught by professional local musicians who volunteer their time. A number of its graduates have gone on to careers in music, while many more continue to enjoy playing an instrument. Thousands of kids from some of Nashville's poorest families have studied at the school.

Natural Nashville

Visitors generally come to Nashville anticipating an urban experience, but that preconception begins to alter even as an airplane
approaches the city. What is visible outside the plane's window are
woods and water. For all its growth, the city still appears from above
like a minor interruption of a vast, green expanse. Mile on mile of
trees, broken only by lakes and rivers. It becomes easy to imagine
how Native Americans from the Choctaw, Cherokee, and Shawnee
tribes found Middle Tennessee so attractive, with its abundance of
fish and game.

The bear and the buffalo are gone, but the woods and waters
still shelter a considerable variety of wildlife. Hundreds of avian
species make Middle Tennessee their home, or pass through during
the course of a year. Fish abound in the lakes and rivers. Of course,
the great outdoors is not always a friendly place for an unwary human.
The tick population—like that in many places across the rest of the
country—is growing, and they can transmit some nasty diseases.
Linen closets are favorite sites for brown recluse spiders, where they
like to live between towels or sheets. Any dark, warm place will do,
and they deliver a nasty—and occasionally fatal—bite when dis-
turbed, as do black widow spiders, which are often found in basements
and sheds. And it's a very good idea to leave the lovely cat-sized
animal in the back yard with its lush black and white fur alone—
skunks will not kill a person, but when they are done spraying, said
person might prefer death.

The eastern rattlesnake is a pretty common resident of the
woods, and recently, rattlers are said to have been found that do not

Surrounded by woods and water.

have a tail with rattles. Evolution is apparently beginning to eliminate this early warning system, since most people who hear it immediately kill the snake in question. Likewise, not all the area's abundant flora is benign. Poison ivy is widespread and extremely unpleasant, depending on a person's degree of sensitivity. The same can be said for poison oak.

Even taking into account all these perils, visitors who do not leave the urban streets to enjoy the great outdoors surrounding the city are missing a large part of the pleasures on offer. To reach most of the city's green spaces, they will need a car, or a friend with a car. Nashvillians have never been willing to vote for funding any sort of mass transit. For decades, virtually the only bus service was early morning and late afternoon on weekdays between the African American neighborhoods of North Nashville and wealthy areas like Belle Meade. This allowed maids and domestics—too poor to own cars—to reach their jobs cleaning houses, tending to the white children during the day, and to get back to their own homes in the evening.

As Nashville has evolved, traffic is a frequently heard complaint from residents, old and new. Despite all that griping, real public transport—intelligently designed to reduce automotive congestion—has never been tried. The citizens have consistently refused to finance it. As recently as May 2018, voters rejected by a 2–1 margin a proposal for a 1 percent sales tax increase, which would have funded five light-rail lines, one Downtown tunnel, four rapid transit bus lines, four new cross-town buses, and more than a dozen transit hubs around the city. Voters opted to stick with their cars.

Carless visitors to Nashville need not be entirely bereft of green space. A number of city parks and greenways are inside the city. Centennial Park, occupying 132 acres (53 ha) behind the campus of Vanderbilt University, was a racetrack from 1884 to 1895, when it was chosen as the site of the 1897 Tennessee Centennial and International Exposition. A life-size replica of the Parthenon was constructed in the park to celebrate the culture and learning of "the Athens of the South." In 1990 a 42-foot (13 m) statue of Pallas Athena, designed by Nashville sculptor Alan LeQuire and executed over an eight-year span, was added to the art gallery inside the Parthenon replica. It is said to be the largest piece of indoor sculpture in the Western world.

The Vanderbilt campus—close by Centennial Park and inaugurated in 1873—is an old-school campus. It has wide, shaded lawns and is full of hundred-year-old trees. Squirrels scamper across the ground, attracting the occasional hawk. Some 190 species of trees can be found on the campus, and it has been designated as a national arboretum site. The oldest survivor is a bur oak, which has been dated to more than two hundred years old, meaning it has been standing since the American revolutionary period.

Even those visitors staying in a Downtown hotel without a car can still find a bit of fresh air to breathe. A pedestrian bridge connects the lower end of Lower Broad with the east bank of the Cumberland River. From there, it's not far to the 336 acres (136 ha) of Shelby Park.

At the end of the nineteenth century, Shelby Park was an amusement park, which went bankrupt and eventually fell into the city's hands. More than a century old, it includes a 1.8-mile (3 km) greenway for walking, as well as space for baseball, fishing, and an eighteen-hole golf course. The greenway is part of a citywide system of walking trails, which was originally conceived as a network of green belts around the city. While they are not all connected, green-ways can be found in most parts of the city.

Once a visitor has an available car, a wealth of nearby natural areas await exploration. On the southern side of the city, just past Belle Meade, are the two Warner Parks, named for the old-money Nashville family who donated the land for public use in 1927. Together, Percy Warner and Edwin Warner parks cover 3,180 acres (1,290 ha) of mostly woods, with over 16 miles (26 km) of hiking trails, along with two nine-hole municipal golf courses, and 10 miles (16 km) of equestrian paths.

Another great alternative for a walk is the man-made Radnor Lake, 8 miles (13 km) south of Downtown. It was dug out in 1913 by the Louisville & Nashville Railroad company to provide water for steam engines. During the late 1960s, the lake and the 1,200 acres (485 ha) surrounding it were bought by a group of private developers, but public pressure resulted in the state's Department of Conservation acquiring the land. The lake is surrounded by some of the highest wooded ridges in Middle Tennessee. Hikers can take one of two basic trails that begin in the parking lot: a flat one that circles in 2.5 miles (4 km) through woods, and along the perimeter of the lake, or the more difficult two-hour trek that climbs the hillside above the lake, and winds along Ganier Ridge. More than 230 species of birds have been identified in the Radnor Lake area, including bald eagles, great horned owls, and blue herons. Animals making it their home include beavers, bobcats, white-tailed deer, minks, muskrats, coyotes, and various species of snake.

For all its flora and fauna, Radnor Lake is diminutive compared to the two vast man-made lakes that are just past the edge of town: Old Hickory and Percy Priest. Warm in the summer and cool in the winter, these lakes cover tens of thousands of acres of farmland that were flooded by the Tennessee Valley Authority to create dams and reservoirs. Old Hickory Lake extends for over 90 miles (145 km), and Percy Priest Lake for 42 miles (68 km).

Nashville is surrounded by plenty of natural wonders, but nature has not always been kind to the city. The most devastating recent example was the great flood of the first week of May 2010. The

Alan LeQuire, *Athena*, in the Parthenon, Centennial Park, unveiled in 1990.

Stones River Greenway.

Cardinal, a year-round Nashville resident.

two-day rain that fell the first week of that month doubled the amount of rain ever received before in a 48-hour period. Meteorologists dubbed it a "thousand-year flood." Eleven people in the Nashville area died. The flood caused more than $2 billion in private property damage, as well as $120 million of destruction to public infrastructure. The mall at Opryland, which is built beside the Cumberland River, was closed for two years following the flood, and the Opryland auditorium was closed for seven months. The waters flooded the basement of the Schermerhorn Symphony Center and ruined many precious instruments stored there, including two Steinway grand pianos, each worth $100,000.

Tornadoes are not uncommon in the city. A bad one roared down Lower Broad and across the river through East Nashville in April 1998, with winds of up to 150 mph (240 kph). It was the first time in twenty years that a major city's Downtown had suffered such a powerful tornado. Three hundred buildings, including the State Capitol, sustained damage. The Tennessee Performing Arts Center had more

Devastation caused by the flood of 2010 (above) and the flood of 1927 (below), which destroyed much of the city's infrastructure.

than a hundred windows blown out. A Vanderbilt University student having a picnic in Centennial Park was killed by a falling tree.

Every century has delivered its handful of devastating natural catastrophes, such as floods, tornados, or ice storms—times when nature's power overwhelmed our ordinary defenses, whether the walls of homes, or the city sewers. But the natural world also makes itself known in Nashville in a less dramatic and more daily fashion. The borders between the natural world and the urban world are surprisingly porous, never hard and fast.

If one drives around Nashville, it pays to be careful, and not just of other drivers. Among the numerous animals routinely crossing the city's streets and yards are possums, raccoons, skunks, and armadillos, the latter almost always found dead on a road, hit by the passing vehicles. Deaf and nearly blind, they did not appear in Middle Tennessee until they arrived from states further south some decades back, but now they account for a lot of Nashville's roadkill. The possums and raccoons like to root around for edibles in human garbage, and they'll make a mess. As if to make amends, possums love to eat ticks, and this makes them valuable to us. People tend to be quite cautious around skunks, but dogs frequently go after them and come home reeking.

The natural world is woven into contemporary suburban living. Cat owners may find one morning that coyotes have taken their pets during the night. Skunks might make a home under the deck. Wasps might build nests in the eaves. The grass lawns are often home to tiny insects called chiggers, which will only bite in their larval, parasitic stage. When they do so, they make a quick munch of some skin cells and drop away from a person's arm or leg, leaving behind an infernally itchy red bite.

Numerous deer move through Nashville, grazing its yards, suburb to suburb. As the late light falls on a cold autumn afternoon, or just at dawn, they drift among the oaks like ghosts in the wisps of fog, four or five in a group. They do not appear to have any aversion to, nor even any caution in, crossing a paved stretch to reach another yard. In 2016 the Tennessee Highway Patrol reported 7,219 deer-related crashes. Of those crashes, 330 involved injuries and one was fatal.

Tennessee buck.

One evening at dusk, I was driving slowly down a winding road in a Nashville suburb, and out of nowhere, a deer was in front of me, filling up my field of vision too suddenly to even brake. One moment my view was a stretch of road, and the next it was the startled face of a full-grown doe looking in at me through the windshield with a panicked expression, as surprised to find herself there as I was. This visual eruption was followed instantly by a solid thump. The deer rolled across the car's hood and into the ditch beside the road, where she staggered to her feet, and stumbled off across a yard. The car was unharmed thanks to the low speed at which I'd been traveling. I pulled over and breathed deeply for a bit until my heart rate slowed.

Drive carefully in those Nashville suburbs with their big sloping lawns, friends. Always assume that a deer is poised to bound out into the middle of the road, and adjust your speed accordingly.

Mary's Old Fashioned Pit Bar-B-Que.

At the Table

Until quite recently, Nashville was not high on the list of cities where a top-notch chef might think about opening a restaurant. In fact, it might not even have been on such a list at all. The city had its own peculiar cuisine, but it was a little hard to love unless you had grown up eating it. Included in white Nashville's favorite foods were things like a pimento cheese sandwich—made of cheddar and cream cheese, chopped red peppers, and mayonnaise on white bread; a fried baloney (or bologna) sandwich; fried pickles; or fried green tomatoes. This kind of food might not be to everyone's taste.

What the city's cooks and chefs did do extremely well was to satisfy local tastes, and they did it using a cuisine drawn from three main sources: the English colonists brought animals such as pigs and chickens, as well as foodstuff such as wheat; the Native American tribes contributed corn and cornbread; and the enslaved Africans brought yams, black-eyed peas, and collard greens.

John Egerton, historian and food activist, described in his *Southern Food* (1987) a New Year's celebration of Southern food that he attended:

> There was the traditional New Year's Day good-luck vegetable, black-eyed peas, cooked with hog jowl and served with rice—an ancient dish somehow pegged with the name hoppin' John—and there was another good-luck food, collard greens. With them on the main table and the sideboards were such time-honored favorites as candied yams, fried okra, green beans, stewed tomatoes, cole slaw, congealed salad, ambrosia,

pan-fried chicken, barbecued pork shoulder, Brunswick stew, smoked fish, roast venison, cornbread and hot biscuits. The drinks ranged from buttermilk to bourbon, and the desserts included pecan and sweet potato and black bottom pies, fudge brownies, and a spectacular snowball icebox cake.

While a patron may not find all of these on a traditional Nashville restaurant menu today, a goodly number of them will be. In addition to the meat-and-three steam tables, the city is home to a host of restaurants featuring barbecue. These places pay varying levels of attention to decor and aesthetics, ranging from none to a lot: from the family-friendly, light and colorful spots, with kitschy art and Coke memorabilia on the walls, to places you enter through a screen door that creaks, where the lighting is poor and the tables all have a folded piece of cardboard under a leg to keep them level. A barbecue sandwich from one of these places, chopped pork topped by coleslaw, a pickle slice, and the cook's homemade sauce on a hamburger bun, is likely to be extremely tasty. There are as many good barbecue places in the South as there are Southerners who want to eat it, and that's plenty of people.

Fried green tomatoes.

The first barbecue sandwich I can remember having was one from Mary's Old Fashioned Pit Bar-B-Que in North Nashville. It was an afterthought—on an occasional Saturday night in the 1960s, my friend got the use of his family car, and we would drive to a particular market in North Nashville, where they were not above selling a six-pack of beer to a scrawny, underage kid like myself, with no fuss about proof of age. One evening, we stopped at Mary's and bought a couple of sandwiches to throw in the brown paper bag with the six cans of Colt .45 malt liquor that my friend and I would take to the drive-in, and sip our way through as we watched a movie. The sandwich was a revelation.

Mary Seals founded the place in the 1950s, and her granddaughter runs it today. No alcohol is served, and no beef either. There is no beef brisket, and for damn sure no hamburgers. Interior decoration is nil. It's a diehard pork place, and a taste of their ribs or a pulled pork sandwich will prove that they are doing right by the pig.

Certain North Nashville eating places like Mary's, which have attracted a steady stream of African American customers for decades, now attract people from all over the city with the food they serve. Mary's is one, and the nearby Swett's, a meat-and-three with a long steam table that has fed North Nashvillians at lunchtime since 1954, is another. For many years both places were favorites of the local African American community, and of a few adventuresome whites from across the tracks, but over the decades, the clientele has definitely diversified. Both places are today patronized by a broad mix of black and white locals, together with a sprinkling of out-of-towners who have read about the eateries online.

It used to be that all barbecue places were uniformly inexpensive and often sparsely decorated. No longer. There are upscale places to eat barbecue, downscale ones, and everything in between. Some barbecue restaurants in today's "It" city will set you back as much as any pretentious bistro serving yuppie delights. Even the readers of glossy magazines such as *Condé Nast Traveler* like to dream about getting their fingers a little greasy and their appetites wholly satisfied. In his wonderful book *Southern Food*, Egerton described barbecue:

It comes minced, chopped, sliced, pulled or clinging to the ribs; on light bread, buns, cornbread, or as an entrée; with sweet, tangy, thick, thin, mild, medium, or hot sauce; topped with cole slaw, onions, pickles, or nothing; accompanied by baked beans, potato salad, sliced tomatoes, corn on the cob, French fries, potato chips, hush puppies . . . In all its myriad combinations, shapes, and tastes, it's a many-splendored comestible with a single name: barbecue (barbeque, Bar-b-q, b-b-q), the smoky, roasted, sauce-doused meat that is second to none as a mouth-watering favorite of Southern eaters.

One hometown favorite that has made it to the national spotlight is hot chicken. Nashville's African American population had been eating it for many years. The story goes that Thornton Prince's wife discovered he was cheating on a Saturday night, and, in retaliation, she prepared a midday Sunday chicken dinner that would scorch the roof of his mouth. It turned out that he loved it, and he wasn't alone. Prince's Hot Chicken Shack opened in 1945, and it thrived. After more than eighty years, it is still run by his descendants, and is currently located out on Nolensville Pike.

Then, suddenly, Prince's hot chicken was being touted around the nation as a marvel of Nashville's cuisine. Foodies such as Anthony Bourdain lauded it. The likes of Beyoncé, Jay-Z, and Jerry Seinfeld were known always to send out for it when they were in Nashville. The James Beard Foundation named Prince's as a 2013 Classic Award winner, noting,

> You can order it from mild (don't be fooled: "mild" is still pretty damn hot), to extra hot . . . The stack of crinkled dill pickle chips and slices of white bread that come with your chicken are the closest things to life rafts your taste buds will find.

Now, a half-dozen hot chicken places are scattered around town competing with Prince's. Hot chicken is basically fried chicken with a cayenne-based paste slathered onto it. A piece of chicken on a hamburger bun usually sells for under $10, with a pickle slice and

Chefs Sean Brock and Erik Anderson visit Prince's Hot Chicken on season two of the television show *The Mind of a Chef*.

some potato salad or coleslaw thrown in. If you like the heat, it's delicious. When hot chicken hit the big time, civic promoters were quick to take advantage of it, and since 2007 an annual Hot Chicken Festival has been held. The Jewish community has even jumped on the hot chicken bandwagon with a Kosher Hot Chicken festival held in November each year.

Apart from hot chicken and other traditional dishes, Nashville now boasts a growing number of places where food is more of an art than a means to simple sustenance. Food writers take note these days of what's on offer from Nashville chefs, and they're not talking classics like barbecue, but sophisticated dishes every bit as imaginative as those found in New York or San Francisco. Up until recently, going out to eat in Nashville did not mean a "dining experience," or spending a lot of money. It meant getting your money's worth of a tasty, filling meal. That is changing. Half a dozen award-winning chefs have opened restaurants over the past few years, and their amazing gastronomic creations are not likely to be served in large portions—or cheaply.

In 2016 chef Tandy Wilson became the city's first James Beard award winner. He had opened his first Downtown restaurant, City House, in December 2007, blazing a trail for other chefs. His choice of location, in Germantown, gave a boost to an inner-city neighborhood in need of revival. Wilson was pretty much a pioneer, but by 2016 he told an interviewer that Nashville had become a town with real culinary imagination and appreciation: "When we first started cooking octopus, everybody—including the entire kitchen—thought I was crazy. And now I think we'd be crazy to take it off the menu. That's where we are now."

Another early promoter of fine dining was The Catbird Seat, opened in 2011 with award-winning Erik Anderson helming the kitchen. The 22-seat restaurant has a U-shaped bar, where diners sit and watch the food being prepared, partaking of a seven-course tasting menu of seasonally inspired dishes. Anderson offered adventurous and well-to-do patrons such dishes as abalone in red-eye gravy, or roasted pigeon with sweetgrass-infused yogurt. He left The Catbird Seat in 2016 to take a head chef position in the kitchen at San Francisco's COI restaurant, which has two Michelin stars.

It's not just high-class dining that has appeared and thrived in the city over the past few years. People still go to meat-and-threes at midday, but the great majority of inexpensive, filling lunches available now are likely to come in flavors that Nashvillians have only come to know in the past couple of decades, foods that would have been as strange thirty years ago as roasted pigeon or octopus. A banh mi sandwich at one of a number of good Vietnamese cafes, or tacos *al pastor* from one of the many food trucks parked around town would not have had many takers.

Nashvillians did form an immediate attachment to food trucks when they began to appear across the city, and they have continued to patronize them. Randall Kenan wrote, in an article titled 'Visible Yam' in *Gravy*, the magazine of the Southern Foodways Alliance,

Nowadays we think of food trucks as a culinary trend . . . But in truth they are as old as cities. Thebes, Athens, Ur, Edo: All had food carts of some fashion. Bringing the food to the people always made good business sense, and we have had the wheel for a good long time.

Farmers' Market, on the downtown Bicentennial Mall.

Currently, many varieties of ethnic food—Vietnamese, Mexican, Kurdish, Indian, Middle Eastern, and Ethiopian—are amply represented in the city's restaurant inventory. White and black Nashvillians are beginning to learn the more subtle differences in ethnic cuisine. Not just "Mexican," but Mexican, Honduran, Colombian, Cuban, El Salvadoran, and Peruvian. Not just "African," but Kenyan, Somalian, and Ethiopian. And not just "Chinese," as Nashvillians used to call any meal associated with the Asian continent, but pho from Vietnam, coconut rice from Thailand, Indian curries, and Korean kimchee.

Even as they have learned to enjoy food from around the globe, Nashvillians have come to have a renewed appreciation of their own indigenous crops. In 1995 a farmers' market was the first thing to open in the newly constructed, open-air Bicentennial Mall, just north of the Capitol, which is now also the site of the new Tennessee State Museum. The market is open year round, and on a busy weekend, some 10,000 people will come through. It has a food court with seventeen different kiosks offering dishes from around the world. Regulations stipulate that the produce on offer has to be sold by the person who grew it. The market carries on a long tradition of farmers selling their produce in the city, which dates back to a farmers' market on the public square in the early 1800s.

The Real Estate Boom

When I was hired to work at Nashville's daily newspaper, *The Tennessean*, during the 1980s, I parked every day at a lot beside the railroad yards behind the abandoned Union Station, where passenger trains no longer called. The area was nicknamed the Gulch. In the heyday of u.s. rail travel, Nashville had been an important interchange, but by the time I went to work only the occasional freight train came through, and the area around the yards was mostly large stretches of empty tracks, and weedy scrub.

During my employment at the newspaper, developers took the beautiful, deserted Romanesque Revival train station—first opened in 1900, and closed in 1979 with the end of passenger train service—and converted it into a luxury hotel, which opened in 1986. It had Italian marble floors, crystal chandeliers, and the original stained-glass lobby ceiling, 65 feet (20 m) high. Nevertheless, the railroad yards behind the hotel remained a desolate expanse of scrub. It was not a place where any people with homes to go to would want to find themselves after the sun went down.

The extensive development of the Downtown, in the first two decades of the twenty-first century, completely changed that. Property in the Gulch is currently far too valuable to stand empty. The area is now home to high-rent residential and office towers, with brightly lit, expensive restaurants and nightspots on the ground floors. The reasons for this dramatic change were familiar ones, appearing again and again across the nation in Downtowns that were abandoned for many years, and then reclaimed by developers. The basic dynamic was that during the postwar years, black

Nashvillians were no longer restricted to North Nashville, and had begun to move into neighborhoods across the city. White people who could afford to do so left for suburbs farther out, and took their amenities—schools, supermarkets, and shopping malls—with them to the edge of town. Many banks, state office buildings, and corporate headquarters remained Downtown, and were full of people working during the day, but by nightfall the employees would be back in the suburbs, and the city center was virtually closed and shuttered.

Generally, the only folks who inhabited Downtown Nashville at night were the homeless. In fact, because of the lack of public transportation, they were pretty much trapped there. A Catholic priest, Charles Strobel, worked on their behalf, and founded Room In The Inn in 1986, a Downtown shelter for homeless men, which provides emergency services, and coordinates the efforts of relief organizations and churches. In 2010 Strobel was the driving force behind the creation of the Campus for Human Development, a three-story building Downtown, which was opened to serve the chronically homeless with basic services on the first floor such as food and medical attention, classrooms on the second floor, and studio apartments on the third. The developers were perfectly happy for the homeless to stay Downtown, pretty much out of the way, while they built out the suburbs.

Since Ronald Reagan began closing institutions for the mentally ill in the 1980s, the number of people experiencing homelessness every year has risen in virtually every city and town in the United States. Most of these people are chronically homeless individuals. But a growing part of the homeless population consists of children who are part of a family experiencing homelessness, often headed by a single mother. Over 2.5 million children were homeless in the u.s. during 2018, and many of their mothers were not in these circumstances for the reasons that keep chronically homeless individuals on the streets—substance abuse, doctors' bills, or mental illness. These families were homeless simply because they could not afford to pay local rental prices. To rent a two-bedroom apartment in any city in the country, and still have enough left over to live, a family needed an annual income of close to $60,000, and lots of single mothers working minimum-wage jobs in Nashville could not get close to having that much money. Homeless mothers in Nashville, as in other cities, tried to keep their families out of sight so that the state wouldn't take their children. They lived packed into the homes of relatives or friends. Those who could scraped together the price of a cheap motel room, one to serve the whole family. A number of extended-stay motels in some of the poorer sections of Nashville served such families. If a single mother could do no better, she and her kids slept in the family car, parked on a dark, out-of-the-way street. Most Nashvillians, even those who worked Downtown on a daily basis, were unaware that more than a thousand children were living among them every day who had nowhere to call home.

Around 1990, the tide of Nashvillians out of the city began to turn. Demand for Downtown living grew strong enough that it caught the attention of urban planners and developers. As in other cities, investors set their sights on Downtown, high-rise, residential development. The market was driven by the usual complaints from young white adults who had grown up in suburbs somewhere: their morning and evening commutes were long and slow; lawn and house maintenance was expensive; to buy even a loaf of bread or a glass of beer, it was necessary to get in the car and drive somewhere, rather than being able to walk.

Unlike a homeless mother with kids, chronically homeless individuals had no motivation to hide themselves. They lived publicly in the streets by day, and were much in evidence when developers began to train their sights on Downtown. For urban settlers coming back to live in the city center, it was impossible to ignore the fact that Nashville had a lot of homeless individuals—by 2018 nearly 3,000 homeless people were counted, and most observers believed that at least that many went uncounted. The first people to move into those new Downtown developments walked softly and warily around the numerous street people, but the newcomers soon learned to pay them no mind. Eventually, the numbers, and buying power, of the new arrivals pretty much overwhelmed the transients, and the high-rises and brightly lit restaurants became Downtown's basic character. In an odd way, the situation had reversed itself with an increasing number of homeless individuals abandoning the inner city to go to the woods that surround Nashville, and live in suburban encampments.

Nevertheless, after abandoning Downtown to the homeless for decades, it has not proven easy to uproot them entirely, as much as developers would like to do so. A recent stark example of this pitted one of Nashville's kingpin real estate developers, Tony Giarratana, against the homeless who gathered, on days when it wasn't raining, with their shopping carts full of belongings in a small pocket park belonging to the city, at Sixth and Church Streets, across from the beautiful main library. As in most cities, the library served as a refuge for homeless people, a warm place where they could read, relax, and use a computer, a rest room, a water fountain. On nice days, and not-so-nice days, some homeless individuals passed much of the day in the park across the street.

Giarratana wanted to put up Nashville's tallest building on that very spot, a 65-story high-rise of condominiums and offices called the Paramount. In 2018 he offered to trade a parking lot he owned on the other side of the State Capitol to the city for the existing pocket park property. The city, he explained, could take the parking lot and turn it into a park for the homeless. It was an out-of-the-way site, where most people would never have to cross paths with the vagrants. Unspoken in his offer to the city, but certainly part of it, was that the land swap would remove a bunch of homeless people from a piece of very valuable property. The city had already taken away most of the benches in the park to make it less comfortable. Because the park had no rest room facilities apart from the library across the street, supporters of Giarratana's plan, which included most Downtown business owners, claimed the park was not only an eyesore, but a public health hazard, and criticized the current park as a "failed public space."

As middle-class people began to move back to the inner city, Nashville's Downtown real estate rose steeply in value. Housing prices skyrocketed. In 2013 the median price of a single-family home reached

$200,000 for the first time. By 2017, it had climbed to $293,000, with a 12.5 percent increase over 2016, the third highest annual increase in the nation. The real estate website Zillow ranked it as the hottest housing market in the entire United States, ahead of cities such as Austin, Texas and Raleigh, North Carolina. While the price of a house was still close to the national average price for urban real estate, and attractive to someone from Los Angeles, San Francisco, Boston, or Manhattan, the fast rise of the real estate market created an affordable housing crisis for those Nashvillians with limited incomes.

In 2018 the nonprofit, nonpartisan Milken Institute put Nashville at number eight among large cities at creating and sustaining jobs. With its strong job market, Nashville became the largest city in the state of Tennessee in 2017, surpassing Memphis by a total of roughly 8,000 people. The folks who were moving to Nashville were just the kind of additions to the local tax base that city officials hoped to see. The city's population of people under 35 with college degrees doubled between 2007 and 2017. Many neighborhoods on both the east and west sides of the Cumberland were full of older, comfortable brick homes with yards and porches. These are now being bought by developers at a furious rate. Often they are torn down,

A tall-and-skinny in west Nashville.

and replaced with McMansions, if they are in a neighborhood where the market will bear a selling price of a million dollars-plus; more often, for homes that sell for less than that, the smaller, older houses are bulldozed and replaced with what are called "tall-and-skinnies." These are narrow, three-story homes with flat facades, which often look like they were constructed from shipping containers piled on top of one another. These tall-and-skinnies are houses that clash with the prior modest brick aesthetic of the neighborhoods, but announce to all that their owners have enough money to build one.

In Midtown Nashville, Vanderbilt University was an early and persistent developer. Beginning in the 1970s, the university has bought and razed numerous blocks of neighborhood residential housing to extend its medical facilities and campus grounds. The university has purchased many millions of dollars of property around it in Midtown. Vanderbilt has an endowment of well over $3 billion, according to the websites that track such things, and it ranks highly on the list of universities with money to spend. The *Nashville Business Journal* reported in 2018 that the university had spent roughly $45

Belmont Mansion.

Alan LeQuire's statue *Musica* used to be the tallest construction on Music Row.

million, or more, buying real estate around the expanding campus since the start of 2014.

Music Row may be the next to fall victim to development. It is a dozen long, tree-shaded blocks of houses, along Sixteenth and Seventeenth Avenues, between Midtown and Downtown, close to Vanderbilt. For decades, Music Row's houses were home to recording studios, publishers, record labels, and the myriad ancillary music industry businesses. The list of bestselling albums in a number of genres recorded in Nashville studios is a long and varied one, and includes B. B. King, Loretta Lynn, Dolly Parton, Elvis Presley, Bob Dylan, Neil Young, Simon and Garfunkel, and the Beach Boys. One end of the Row is anchored by Belmont University, and the other end by a traffic circle, in the middle of which is Alan LeQuire's 38-foot-tall (12 m) bronze statue *Musica*, which features nine naked life-size dancers. They are atop a knoll in the middle of the traffic circle, resting on a base of bronze and massive boulders of local limestone. The dancers celebrate the importance of the neighborhood's music industry to the city, according to the sculptor.

Music Row's signature presence is rapidly being erased, as Vanderbilt and the city's other big developers cast an eye on those long, quiet blocks of valuable real estate. Between 2014 and 2017, some 43 Music Row buildings were bought and demolished so that properties could be developed. Hotels and office towers have proliferated. Each year, a nonprofit preservationist group, Historic Nashville, Inc., issues a list it calls "The Nashville Nine," which are the nine most endangered historic properties in the city. Each year, there are plenty of candidates, but in 2018 five of the Nashville Nine were located on Music Row.

Literary and Artistic Nashville

"Nashville appears quite often in my work, and I can't write fiction at all except about the South."
Robert Penn Warren

The city has long been known as a book-lover's town, and throughout its history, the written word has always played an important role. The first publishing houses were present in the early nineteenth century, and in the twenty-first century, the publishing arm of the United Methodist Church was headquartered in Nashville, as was the less staid and more apocalyptic-minded Christian publisher Thomas Nelson, in addition to Lifeway, the publishing arm of the Southern Baptist Convention.

Bookstores, too, have been present since the beginning of the nineteenth century, when they often combined the duties of stationers, sales of playing cards and dice to gamblers, rental libraries, and letterpress printing. Independent bookstores thrived there until the 1990s, when the big-box chains forced the independents out of business, and it looked like Nashville might lose its locally owned bookstores. Then the chains themselves were forced out of business by Amazon and other online retailers following the rise of Internet shopping. In 2011 best-selling novelist Ann Patchett came back to her hometown and opened Parnassus Books in the upscale Green Hills neighborhood, rekindling the city's regard for independent booksellers. Patchett said in an interview when the store opened in 2011,

> We've all had the experience of going into a three-story Barnes & Noble and saying, "I didn't really find anything I wanted to read." But you can go in to a small store with an intelligent staff

Ann Patchett at Le Conversazioni, Rome, 2015.

. . . [and] well-displayed, well-chosen books, and come out with five books that you're dying to read. And that's what we're going to do.

Another fine book-lover's independent bookstore is across the river in East Nashville. The Bookshop was opened in mid-2016 and stocks only those books recommended by its owner, Joelle Herr, who grew up just outside of Nashville. Alkebu-Lan Images Bookstore is an excellent, welcoming, African American bookstore, which opened in 1986, close to the Tennessee State University campus. These independent bookstores have injected a blast of energy into Nashville's literary scene. They offer readings by nationally known authors and a relaxed ambience that caters to readers.

More readings and book-centered events take place at the Ben West Public Library, in the heart of Downtown at Seventh and Church. It is the main public library, and it is amply housed in a vast and lovely modern classical stone building. It offers year-round readings and public meeting spaces. The library features a wonderful Civil Rights room, with books about Nashville's role in integrating the South, as well as some interesting videos about those years, which are available for viewing on site. It also has a Nashville Room, with an extensive collection of books about the city.

Every first weekend of October, the Southern Festival of Books is held, with publishers selling their wares on Legislative Plaza while readings are given in the state legislature's chambers. The festival draws hundreds of authors from around the country, and tens of thousands of book lovers, for a weekend celebration of the written word. Nashville also has its share of resident writers. In addition to Ann Patchett, Alice Randall pens both novels and country songs. In 1994 Trisha Yearwood had a number-one country hit with a song Randall co-wrote, and in 2001 her parody of *Gone with the Wind*, called *The Wind Done Gone*, was a *New York Times* bestseller. Among other writers making Nashville their home are Adam Ross, J. T. Ellison, Brad Thor, and Andrew Maraniss, along with poets such as Mark Jarman and Tom House.

Historically, the city has produced its share of notable writers. Robert Penn Warren is the 1947 Pulitzer Prize-winning author of the novel *All the King's Men*, and later served as the nation's first poet laureate. He also won Pulitzers in 1958 and 1979 for his poetry,

Ben West Library courtyard.

becoming the only author who has ever won the prize for both fiction and poetry.

In addition to the written word, the city has an active visual arts community, with a long history on both sides of the tracks. William Edmondson was a modest carver of gravestones who—in 1937—became the first African American to have a solo exhibition at New York's Museum of Modern Art. His parents had been slaves in Nashville, owned by a man named H. William Compton. After emancipation, they stayed on the plantation until their ex-master died. William Edmondson was born around 1874. The family eventually left the farm and moved into the Edgehill neighborhood, the equivalent of a black suburb, just south of Black Bottom. Edmondson worked as a gravestone carver for decades before he had a vision in which God told him to begin sculpting. He worked in Nashville's

William Edmondson, *Boxer*, c. 1936.

Consuelo Kanaga, *William Edmondson*, 1950, gelatin silver photograph.

limestone, carving out animals, angels, and figures, doing what he believed God had put him on earth to do.

Aaron Douglas, a painter, was another important African American artist. Scholars have called him "the father of black American art." He was an important figure in the Harlem Renaissance, before taking a position as head of Fisk University's art department in 1944, which he held for 22 years. His obituary in the *New York Times* in February 1979 noted that he assumed "leadership among black artists in the '20s and '30s at a time when critical conceptual decisions were being made by black artists, writers and philosophers."

Television host Oprah Winfrey, one of the most influential African American women in the country, came to North Nashville as a young teenager to live with her father, leaving behind an abusive mother in Milwaukee. She thrived in Nashville, winning oratorical contests and attending the predominantly black Tennessee State University and majoring in Communication. She received her first media job at seventeen years old, when she began delivering the news on wvol radio. She considers herself a Nashvillian, and the city is proud to claim her.

Betsy Graves Reyneau,
portrait of Aaron Douglas,
c. 1943–63.

The well-known and colorful multimedia artist Red Grooms was born and raised in Nashville. Born in 1937, Grooms has had his work has hung in museums such as the Museum of Modern Art and the Whitney Museum of American Art in New York. Grooms built a large carousel for Nashville's first Riverfront Park project. The carousel featured Grooms-ian portraits of 36 noted Tennessee figures, and in 1998 it was unveiled in the park to great fanfare. Grooms came down from his Manhattan home, and Senator Bill Frist was on hand to do the honors. Within a few years, however, the park's attendance had declined, the carousel needed repair, and it was dismantled and stored in a West Nashville warehouse. This saved it, no doubt, from being destroyed in the 2010 flood, which covered the riverfront. Since then, community efforts have been mounted to bring the carousel out of storage and install it somewhere to be seen and enjoyed, but as of yet, it has not been resurrected.

In 2000 Nashville instituted a "one-percent-for-art" policy, by which 1 percent of bond proceeds from certain capital projects would be earmarked for public art. The policy's effects are visible in many places around the city, from the massive, red, flowing steel sculpture by Alice Aycock on the Cumberland's east bank, titled *Ghost Ballet for the East Bank Machineworks*, to the haunting fifteen-story mural on a towering, abandoned concrete silo in the Nations neighborhood of West Nashville, painted by Australian artist Guido van Helten. On one side is a portrait of a 91-year-old man who had lived in the neighborhood since the 1920s, and who represents the past. On another side are two young children, who are the future.

Oprah Winfrey, at age nineteen, reading the news on the air at WVOL, 1973.

Alice Aycock, *Ghost Ballet for the East Bank Machineworks*, 2007, steel, neon, aluminum, and industrial metals. This piece is a representation of the transformation of the East Bank from an industrial area to a site for recreation and play.

Van Helten is Australian, but he spent some time in West Nashville's Nations community, where tall-and-skinnies are now proliferating. In an interview in 2018, he spoke of the 91-year-old Lee Estes, a lifelong neighborhood resident, who was the model for the mural.

To me he stands symbolic against the inevitable tide of gentrification. This is an issue that in some cases has left the underprivileged in worse positions, as developers and real estate agents move to capitalize on the Nashville housing boom.

Many murals, paintings, sculptures, and installations have been placed in public spaces, thanks to the one-percent-for-art policy. Millions of dollars have been collected and spent on more than fifty pieces of public art across the city. An online map is available, identifying 36 sites where art is on public display.

Silo mural by Guido van Helten.

Mural by Beau Stanton on
Fifth Ave. N. honoring Middle
Tennessee waterways.

Burning Las Vegas rocking the house at BB King's Blues Club.

Nighttime's the Right Time

Nashville's metamorphosis into a big city has transformed the city's nightlife. Whereas in my youth, the strip clubs in Printer's Alley were about the pinnacle of a night on the town, currently all kinds of evening activities are on offer, ranging from independent films, to elegant, staid hotel bars, honky-tonks, jazz clubs, blues venues, and sports bars.

Film fans may have it best. The period after the Second World War saw a boom in theaters. Nashvillians turned out in force for the latest Hollywood hits. Until Downtown was utterly abandoned in the late 1980s, huge, elegant movie theaters there thrived. There were three on Church Street alone, including the Tennessee Theater, opened in 1952 in an art deco shell of a building first constructed in 1932. The Tennessee lasted until 1988, when it became the last of the Church Street theaters to close.

The suburbs had their own cinema palaces. The elegant Belle Meade Theater opened in 1940, with 1,100 seats, and it had a Wall of Fame with signed portraits of many of Hollywood's most famous stars who had visited the theater. The Green Hills Theater, on Hillsboro Road, opened in 1951, and had a "crying room" lined with sound-proof glass, where children could be deposited by parents so they didn't have to hire a babysitter if they wanted to go to the movies. These days, people who want Hollywood blockbusters go to multiplex theaters in shopping malls.

For devotees of independent films, there is the Belcourt Cinema in Hillsboro Village. It began life as a movie theater in 1925, when it opened showing silent movies with a Kimball organ providing soundtracks, eight hundred leather-covered seats, and the largest stage in Nashville. It was the stage that kept the place in business: from 1934 to 1936, it was the site of the Grand Ole Opry, before that show moved to the Ryman. Then the Belcourt served as a community theater through the 1950s. In 1966 new owners began showing movies there again.

That lasted until 1999, when the Internet's rise, along with DVD rentals, resulted in falling attendance, and the theater was closed. In 2003 it reopened under the stewardship of a nonprofit group, which eventually replaced the dilapidated seating, undertook major renovations of the building, and installed the latest high-tech projection equipment. The Belcourt is dedicated to bringing independent and documentary films to Nashville's moviegoers, and they have done a superb job.

While homosexuals in postwar Nashville were deep in the public closet, a handful of venues served as gathering places. A woman named Juanita Brazier opened a beer bar, Juanita's, Downtown at Seventh and Commerce in 1952. "When she first opened they'd come

Lobby of the Tennessee Theater, razed in 1988.

Belcourt Theater in Hillsboro Village, 2016.

in the bar and raid her, and take everyone down," Joyce Riley, a former manager at Juanita's, told me in 1987. "They almost drove her out, but she talked to the chief of police and asked him why these people couldn't have a place to drink together?"

The chief decided to come and see the place for himself, Joyce Riley remembered.

[Juanita] had a sign on the restroom door that said, "One at a time." When the chief came in and saw the sign he told her that as long as people didn't wear short shorts and kept their hands to themselves it was okay, and after that they left her alone. Whenever she'd leave in the evening she'd tell everyone, "Goodbye, and keep your hands on the table."

These days the police have other fish to fry, and the gay community gathers pretty much wherever it wants. Church Street has a pair of gay-friendly dance clubs, Play and Tribe, and it is not hard to find other gay venues around town. While these places cater primarily to a gay clientele, most of them are inclusive, and no one is barred for being straight.

Where you're not likely to see same-sex couples dancing is Lower Broad, with its tourist honky-tonks and clubs catering to a line-dancing, two-stepping crowd. They are inclusive only in the sense that dancers have widely varying degrees of proficiency. Some are fluid and practiced, while other couples seem to be taking the floor for the first time, shuffling more than dancing. But the music is perfect for moving, and it's hard to stay seated in these places.

The music in the Latin clubs around town is also moving, but in those places, you had better know what you're doing when you step out to dance to bachata, cumbia, reggaeton, and the other rhythms on the menu at the city's dance clubs favored by the Hispanic population. But who needs to dance at these places? Just sitting with a drink on the table and watching the elegant and graceful dancers, who know what they're doing, is a pleasure.

The Nashville Predators have brought major-league ice hockey to Nashville.

Tennessee Performing Arts Center.

For those who prefer to sit and listen to a different kind of music, Nashville even has jazz venues. For years, session musicians from the country music studios who liked to play jazz had to gather in their off-hours at someone's house to play for the sheer pleasure of it. Finally, jazz is getting some respect. The Nashville Jazz Workshop is a Downtown treat for jazz buffs and those who want to study the music, offering a range of classes and workshops, and weekend gigs by some of the city's best.

For more-sedate but no-less-pleasing musical evenings, there are the Nashville Symphony Orchestra's numerous concerts at the Schermerhorn Symphony Center, as well as the Blair School of Music's regular offerings during the academic year in the school's acoustically outstanding auditorium on the Vanderbilt University campus.

The music that the majority of people in Nashville want to hear is, of course, none of the above, but is instead country and western. In addition to the live music in the Downtown honky-tonks and dance palaces, and bars across the city, the Grand Ole Opry still counts some of the finest country performers in the world on its

Saturday night roster. It's not cheap, with most tickets starting at around $75, but it's a night that country fans will never forget.

Even for those who are not ice hockey fans, an evening spent at Bridgestone Arena for a home game of the top-flight, National Hockey League team, the Nashville Predators, is an exciting experience. The arena holds more than 17,000 people when it is sold out, which it usually is for a Predators match. Although it is a long way from the frozen North, Nashville's ice hockey fans tend towards rabid enthusiasm, and the city's ice hockey savvy has grown exponentially since the team came to the city in 1998.

Downtown, within walking distance of Lower Broad, the Tennessee Performing Arts Center, a large venue across Sixth Avenue North from Legislative Plaza, holds three auditoriums, which often present touring Broadway shows, dance, drama, and musical performances, as well as local productions. It is home to three resident companies, the Nashville Ballet, Nashville Opera, and Nashville Repertory Theatre.

LISTINGS

Hotels

Hermitage
231 Sixth Avenue North
www.thehermitagehotel.com
Opened in its Downtown location in 1910, the Hermitage is still the
most elegant hotel in town, with its period furnishings and up-to-date
amenities. Its restaurant, the Capitol Grille, bills itself as the oldest
Southern-style restaurant in Tennessee, and its vegetables come from
its own Middle Tennessee farm.

Dream—Nashville Printer's Alley
210 Fourth Avenue North
www.dreamhotels.com
In the heart of Printer's Alley Downtown, fifteen minutes from the
airport and walking distance from attractions such as the Country
Music Hall of Fame. The rooms are art deco in style, and the
GuestHouse presidential suite features a microbrew on tap and
a mahogany poker table. The Terrace Suite has a barbecue grill
and a barbecue butler on call.

Union Station Hotel
1001 Broadway
www.unionstationhotelnashville.com
The Romanesque Revival architecture of the former train station, with
its 65-foot (20 m) vaulted stained-glass ceiling in the lobby, is currently
the Marriott chain's premiere Downtown offering. Next door to the
Frist Contemporary Art Museum, and only a few blocks away from
Lower Broad and its honky-tonks, it is a part of Nashville's history.

Noelle
200 Fourth Avenue North
www.noelle-nashville.com
A 224-room boutique hotel on the site of the original Noel Hotel, which
was opened in 1929 in the heart of Downtown, and across the street
from the Arcade. The latest iteration utilizes local creative talent to

design and decorate its rooms. The Rare Bird rooftop terrace bar offers a bird's-eye view of the city.

Gaylord Opryland Resort and Convention Center

2800 Opryland Drive

www.marriott.com

Currently owned by Marriott, the Opryland Resort has 9 acres (3.6 ha) of lush gardens, cascading waterfalls, dining areas, and a water park. The Grand Ole Opry performs next door every Saturday night. There is an 18-hole golf course, and with 2,882 guest rooms and suites, it is one of the nation's largest hotels.

Watering Holes

Oak Bar

231 Sixth Avenue North

www.capitolgrillenashville.com

When the Hermitage Hotel opened in 1910, it was a private gentlemen's club. While its admission policy is now inclusive, its wood paneling and comfortable furnishings evoke the staid tranquility of its roots. The bar claims Nashville's largest selection of bourbons, offering some 130 different examples of the distiller's art. A good place to talk business or love.

The Stage on Broadway

412 Broadway

www.thestageonbroadway.com

If you want live, well-played country music, a place to dance to it, lots of tourists whooping it up, and plenty of beer and whisky, look no further. Forget having a quiet conversation here, this is Lower Broad at its most raucous, but it's also lively, low-lit, and plenty of fun.

Dee's Country Cocktail Lounge

102 East Palestine Avenue, Madison, TN

https://deeslounge.com

This place, located just past Nashville's eastern border, offers music, drink, and hot food. Opened in 2017, owner Amy Dee decided to create a "dive bar" atmosphere that would evoke the 1970s. She succeeded, and it feels like Dee's has been here for decades, with a down-home decor that draws locals and visitors alike.

Pinewood Social

33 Peabody Street

www.pinewoodsocial.com

This unusual combination of bar, restaurant, and bowling alley offers craft cocktails, a substantial menu, and six full-size bowling lanes that are rented by the hour. Come for supper, an after-dinner drink, and a couple of hours bowling, and you've had a varied evening all in the same spot.

Skull's Rainbow Room

222 Printer's Alley

www.skullsrainbowroom.com

David "Skull" Schulman opened Skull's Rainbow Room in 1948, in Printer's Alley. A local eccentric, Skull was often seen around town in rainbow-colored overalls walking his poodles—Elvis Presley gave him one. Skull was known always to have a large wad of cash in his pocket. He was murdered in his club at the age of eighty, in 1998, by a pair of itinerant carnival workers. The club he founded continues, offering a full dinner menu, craft cocktails and live jazz and blues performances, as well as a nightly burlesque show, harking back to the Alley's glory days.

The Patterson House

1711 Division Street

www.thepattersonnashville.com

Opened in 2009, the Patterson House's decor is strictly speakeasy, in a superbly designed space. This is a place where wonderfully crafted cocktails are what counts, and a number of rules are enforced here to assure that's what happens. No cell phone conversations are allowed, and men are not permitted to speak to women they do not know.

No. 308

407 Gallatin Avenue

http://bar308.com

Bars of every stripe can be found along East Nashville's Gallatin Avenue, but this one stands out with its hipster vibe and excellent cocktails. Opened in 2010, some of its creations are named after Beat writers such as William Burroughs, Jack Kerouac, Richard Brautigan, and Charles Bukowski. A DJ plays once a week, and is always relaxed and inviting.

Hops & Crafts

319 Twelfth Avenue South

www.hopscrafts.com

Nashville is a beer lover's town, where local brewmeisters have been at work since the 1980s. This bar was opened in 2013, in one of Nashville's hippest neighborhoods, and offers 36 craft beers, ranging from IPAs to stouts so strong that if you spill them on the floor, you can pick them up and put them back in the glass (just kidding!).

Restaurants

Acme Feed & Seed

101 Broadway

www.acmefeedandseed.com

For decades, farmers patronized this place at the lowest point of Lower Broad to buy feed for their cows and chickens, and seed to plant. Now the first floor offers eclectic dining, the second a bar and lounge, the third a music and dance space, and, above it all, the rooftop patio, with a spectacular view of the city.

Arnold's Country Kitchen

605 Eighth Avenue South

www.arnoldscountrykitchen.com

Begun as a humble Downtown cafeteria in the early 1980s, this family-owned restaurant is one of the city's iconic meat-and-three spots. It features Southern cooking at its best, with everything from fried green tomatoes to chess pie. Arnold's is only open for lunch, and there is always a line waiting to reach the steam tables, but almost everyone in that line will tell you the wait is worth it.

Swett's

2725 Clifton Avenue

http://swettsrestaurant.com

Another wonderful meat-and-three restaurant, open since 1954. For under $10, diners can heap their plates with superb Southern cuisine. This North Nashville gem used to be mainly patronized by African American Nashvillians from the neighborhood, but now people come from all across the city to eat there. It's open for lunch and supper until 8 p.m.

Midtown Cafe

102 Nineteenth Avenue South

www.midtowncafe.com

A favorite of both locals and visitors, Midtown Cafe is open for breakfast, lunch, and dinner, serving an American menu of items such as steak, shrimp, meatloaf, and crab cakes. Located next to Music Row and Vanderbilt University on one side, and Downtown on the other, it offers a free shuttle to hotels and nearby residences.

The Catbird Seat

1711 Division Street

www.thecatbirdseatrestaurant.com

This is award-winning high-cuisine at its best. The restaurant seats only 23 patrons, and it does so around a U-shaped counter surrounding the chefs, whose every move can be watched. Because it's so small, reservations need to be made at least a month in advance. The cuisine is chef-driven and innovative—American with Japanese and Italian influences, featuring dishes like sake-marinated cauliflower.

City House
1222 Fourth Avenue North
https://cityhousenashville.com
Only dinner is served at chef Tandy Wilson's James Beard-award-winning restaurant in the Germantown neighborhood. It was opened in 2007 in the former studio of sculptor Alan LeQuire, and was a pioneer in bringing a different approach to traditional ingredients. The food is Southern, fused with Italian. Artisan pizzas featuring locally sourced ingredients and imaginative takes on standard dishes make it a local favorite.

Etch
303 Demonbreun Street
https://etchrestaurant.com
Chef Deb Paquette was the first woman in Tennessee to be certified as an executive chef, and at Etch, it's easy to see she deserved it. Opened in 2012, serving lunch and dinner, it's not cheap, but Paquette's superb dishes such as the octopus and shrimp bruschetta, lamb loin, or signature roasted cauliflower with truffled pea purée, salted almonds, feta crema, and red bell pepper sauce make it well worth the money.

Museums and Galleries

Frist Art Museum
919 Broadway
https://fristartmuseum.org
The Frist Art Museum, opened in 2001, is housed in an elegant white-marble, art deco building, which was opened in 1935 as the main post office, and was connected by a tunnel to Union Station next door to move the mail more rapidly. The Frist is a non-collecting entity, hosting important traveling exhibitions of well-known artists, bringing art to the community and the community to art.

Cheekwood Estate and Gardens

1200 Forrest Park Drive

https://cheekwood.org

The Cheek family's estate, a Regency-style home on 55 acres (22 ha), less than a mile (1.5 km) past the elegant Belle Meade neighborhood, was opened as Cheekwood Botanical Garden and Museum of Art in 1960. The nineteenth-century mansion holds the museum's six hundred works of American art, including a small, but high-quality, collection of late twentieth-century artists such as Andy Warhol, Larry Rivers, and Red Grooms, as well as the world's largest collection of work by the Nashville stone sculptor William Edmondson.

Carl Van Vechten Gallery

1000 Seventeenth Avenue North

www.fiskuniversitygalleries.org

The Van Vechten Gallery at Fisk University is home to the Alfred Stieglitz modern art collection, with works by Pablo Picasso, Paul Cézanne, Renoir, Diego Rivera, and Georgia O'Keefe. The gallery is named in honor of Carl Van Vechten, a wealthy New York patron of African American artists and writers, who was instrumental in obtaining Stieglitz's collection for Fisk. Also in Fisk's collection are a number of important African American artists, as part of the two hundred works in the Harmon collection, with many of the leading African American and African artists of the early to mid-twentieth century.

Country Music Hall of Fame and Museum

222 Fifth Avenue South

https://countrymusichalloffame.org

The museum, accredited since 1987, likes to call itself the "Smithsonian of country music." Its 350,000 ft² (32,500 m²) building houses an ample and impressive permanent collection of some 2 million items documenting the history and growth of country music. The museum features temporary exhibitions, and has its own reissue record label and book publishing arms.

Tennessee State Museum
1000 Rosa L. Parks Boulevard
https://tnmuseum.org
In 2018 the Tennessee State Museum moved to a new building beside the Farmers' Market. With a spectacular view of Downtown from the second floor, it has a permanent collection of paintings, objects, and videos documenting the state's history, as well as spaces for temporary exhibitions.

LeQuire Gallery
4304 Charlotte Avenue
www.lequiregallery.com
Opened in 2003 by figurative sculptor and lifelong Nashvillian Alan LeQuire, and located in the hip Charlotte Avenue part of West Nashville, this ample space showcases a wide variety of excellent sculptors, painters, wood carvers, and ceramicists. It also houses LeQuire's studio and features a wide selection of his work.

The Arts Company
215 Fifth Avenue North
www.theartscompany.com
Downtown now has a number of art galleries, both in the Arcade and the streets around it, but the Arts Company on Fifth Avenue North was the pioneer. Founded in 1996 by longtime Nashville arts promoter Anne Brown, it still represents some of Nashville's best artists and photographers.

Shopping

A. J. Martin
2817 West End Avenue
https://ajmartinonline.com
Nobody else in town quite has A. J.'s eagle eye for beautiful antique jewelry, nor her imagination in designing new art deco- and Edwardian-style pieces. Both the old and the new are on ample

display at her store. Check out the Red Grooms paintings along the upper walls.

Alkebu-Lan Images Bookstore

2721 Jefferson Street

www.facebook.com/AlkebulanImages

This African American bookstore opened in 1986 with a wide selection of reading for both adults and children, plus gifts, art, and clothes, all Afrocentric, in a welcoming, inclusive Jefferson Street store. The store also hosts frequent readings by black authors, and a wide range of educational events.

Parnassus Books

3900 Hillsboro Pike #14

www.parnassusbooks.net

This independent bookstore, begun in 2011 and co-owned by novelist Ann Patchett, is a place where readers are respected and get the attention they deserve. It provides book shopping as it should be, with a staff who love books. The store hosts regular readings by some of the nation's leading authors.

Plaza Mariachi

3955 Nolensville Pike

https://plazamariachi.com

A shopping mall with a distinctly Latin flavor, where food, drink, clothes, and gifts all have their roots south of Texas. Located in a former mega-supermarket, ten restaurants offer a variety of Latin food. Since the early 1990s, the Nolensville Pike area has been home to a large Latin population, many first-generation families from Mexico, Honduras, El Salvador, the Dominican Republic, Colombia, and so on.

Scarlett Begonia

2805 West End Avenue

http://scarlettassociates.shoplightspeed.com

Founded in 1981 by a couple who had lived in Central and South America, and currently managed by their daughter, Scarlett Begonia sells clothing and all kinds of things from these and other foreign locales, focusing on fair trade, artisanal, and eco-friendly products.

Ernest Tubb Record Shop

417 Broadway

https://etrecordshop.com

The Ernest Tubb Record Shop was on Lower Broad selling country music records long before the first tsunami of tourists arrived. A landmark for devotees of the genre, it was opened in 1947 by the recording artist Ernest Tubb. His tour bus, nicknamed the Green Hornet, was used to transport Ernest Tubb and the Texas Troubadours to gigs across the Southland and is now on view inside the store's branch in Music Valley Village, across from Opryland.

Batch Gift Shop

900 Rosa L. Parks Boulevard

https://batchusa.com

Everything in this small Downtown shop is connected to Nashville in some way, with roots in Southern soil, and the inventory covers a lot of ground. Edibles include the iconic Goo Goo Clusters chocolate and peanut combination, as well as books, jewelry, toys, and knick-knacks, all with a local connection.

Frye Boot Store

401 Eleventh Avenue South

www.thefryecompany.com

Founded in 1863 in Massachusetts, Frye Boot Store is the oldest continuously operated boot company in the U.S., offering a wide range for men, women, and children, from cowboy to cold-weather boots, and it has an extensive online presence. The 3,000 ft² (280 m²) store opened in 2016 in the Gulch and marked an impressive entrance into the Nashville market.

Hatch Show Print

224 5th Avenue South

https://hatchshowprint.com

For well over a century, this print shop has been using letterpress techniques to print posters and handbills for upcoming concerts and shows. Their inventory offers very reasonably priced copies, ready for framing, of some great circus and music posters. For most of its life it was located on Lower Broad, but it is now part of the Country Music Hall of Fame.

Chronology

1779 The first white settlers arrive across the mountains from North Carolina and build Fort Nashborough on the banks of the Cumberland River

1783 Chickasaw chiefs sign a peace treaty with James Robertson and company, although Cherokee and Creek tribes refuse to sign

1784 Nashville is established

1792 The Battle of the Bluffs takes place

1796 The Nashville settlement joins the state of Tennessee and the Union of the United States

1804 Andrew Jackson acquires the land for his plantation, where he would build the Hermitage

1806 Nashville is incorporated as a city; the first mayoral election takes place

1807 The Bank of Nashville is chartered

1811 An earthquake along the New Madrid Fault shakes Nashville houses

1812 The War of 1812 takes place; Tennessee's General Assembly moves to Nashville

1816 The Nashville Female Academy is founded

1819 The first steamboat arrives at Nashville

1822 Nashville's first public cemetery, the Nashville City Cemetery, opens

1823 The first bridge across the Cumberland opens

1824 Andrew Jackson runs for president and loses to John Quincy Adams

1826 Tennessee's state capital moved to Nashville

1827 Quinine is introduced to Nashville to treat malaria

1828 Andrew Jackson wins the presidential election against John Quincy Adams by a landslide

1830 President Jackson calls for and signs Indian removal legislation

1843 Nashville officially becomes the state capital of Tennessee

1850 The Adelphi Theatre is opened; the important suspension bridge across the Cumberland River opens at the site of today's Woodland Street Bridge

1859 The Tennessee State Capitol is completed by Francis Strickland, after the death of the original architect, his father William, in 1854; Louisville & Nashville Railroad opens

1861 The Civil War begins

1862 Union forces occupy Nashville

1864 The Battle of Nashville takes place

1865 The Civil War ends; Nashville's slaves are freed; Fisk University opens as a women's college

1869 The Maxwell House Hotel opens

1871 The Fisk Jubilee Singers is founded

1873   Vanderbilt University opens

1873   A cholera epidemic in which nearly 1,000 die

1874   Nashville's first Jewish synagogue is inaugurated

1876   The *Nashville Banner* newspaper begins publishing

1892   The Union Gospel Tabernacle, later renamed the Ryman
        Auditorium, is built

1897   Centennial Park is created to host the Centennial Exposition;
        a full-scale Parthenon replica is built for it

1906   The first Tennessee State Fair is held

1907   The *Nashville Tennessean* newspaper begins publication

1910   The Hermitage Hotel opens

1918   The Dutchman's Curve train wreck occurs;
        The Spanish influenza epidemic strikes Nashville

1925   WSM radio begins broadcasting the Grand Ole Opry

1927   Edwin Warner Park and Percy Warner Park open

1936   Berry Field, Nashville's first airport, is inaugurated

1937   The Tennessee State Museum opens

1946   The Nashville Symphony plays its first concert

1950   Nashville's first television station begins broadcasting

1951   Ben West is elected mayor, in office during civil rights struggle

1952   The Tennessee Theatre opens

1957   The Life & Casualty (L&C) Tower is built

1960   Anti-segregation sit-ins begin

1963   Nashville and Davidson County join to form one government

1974   The Grand Ole Opry moves from the Ryman to Opryland

1975   Robert Altman's film *Nashville* opens in cinemas

1980   The Tennessee Performing Arts Center opens

1983   Riverfront Park opens

1987   Nashville International Airport opens

1988   The first Southern Festival of Books takes place

1994   Zoning changes permit residential development Downtown

1996   The Bicentennial Mall and Bridgestone Arena open

1998   A powerful tornado rips through Downtown and East Nashville, damaging more than three hundred buildings

2001   The Frist Center for the Visual Arts, the new Country Music Hall of Fame, and the new Downtown Nashville Public Library open

2006   The Schermerhorn Symphony Center opens

2010   Flooding in Nashville and Davidson County kills eleven people and causes an estimated $2 billion in property damage

2011   Parnassus Books opens

2012 The first season of television series *Nashville* airs

2013 The *New York Times* declares Nashville an "It" city

2017 Every day more than one hundred newcomers are recorded to have arrived

2018 British Airways inaugurates nonstop flights between Nashville and London, and new Tennessee State Museum building opens

Suggested Reading and Viewing

Books

Bell, Madison Smartt, *Soldier's Joy* (New York, 1989)

Brandt, Robert, *Natural Nashville: A Guide to the Greenways and Nature Parks* (Nashville, TN, 2013)

Burt, Jesse, *Nashville: Its Life and Times* (Nashville, TN, 1959)

Corlew, Robert E., and William B. Wheeler, *Tennessee: The Volunteer State* (Sun Valley, CA, 2008)

Crabb, Alfred Leland, *Nashville: Personality of a City* (New York, 1960)

Crutchfield, James A., *On this Day: A Brief History of Nashville and Middle Tennessee* (Franklin, TN, 1995)

Dean, Karl, and Michael Kass, *Nashville: The South's New Metropolis* (Nashville, TN, 2016)

Dorman, Lee, *Nashville Broadcasting* (Charleston, SC, 2009)

Doyle, Don, *New Men, New Cities, New South: Atlanta, Nashville, Charleston, Mobile, 1860–1910* (Chapel Hill, NC, 1990)

—, *Nashville in the New South: 1890–1930* (Knoxville, TN, 1985)

Egerton, John, ed., *Nashville: An American Self-portrait* (Nashville, TN, 2011)

—, *Southern Food* (New York, 1987)

—, ed., *Nashville: The Faces of Two Centuries, 1780–1980* (Nashville, TN, 1979)

Franklin, John Hope, and Loren Schweninger, *In Search of the Promised Land: A Slave Family in the Old South* (New York, 2006)

Goodstein, Anita Shafer, *Nashville, 1780–1860: From Frontier to City* (Gainesville, FL, 1989)

Grzybicki, Kerri, *The Nashville Guide* (Nashville, TN, 2017)

Halberstam, David, *The Children* (New York, 1998)

Hoobler, James, *Art Work of Nashville, 1894–1901* [index of historic sites] (Nashville, TN, 1984)

Kreyling, Christine, "Nashville Past and Present," 2005, www.sitemason.com

Lauder, Kathy, and Mike Slate, eds, *From Knickers to Body Stockings and Other Essays from the Nashville Historical Newsletter* (Nashville, TN, 2006)

Lovett, Bobby L., *The African American History of Nashville, Tennessee, 1780–1930* (Fayetteville, AR, 1999)

Maslowski, Peter, *Treason Must Be Made Odious: Military Occupation and Wartime Reconstruction in Nashville, Tennessee, 1862–65* (Millwood, NY, 1978)

Netherton, John, and Martha Weesner, eds, *Tennessee: A Homecoming* (Nashville, TN, 1985)

Patchett, Ann, et al., *Scenes from the New American South* (New York, 2018)

Schweid, Richard, *Invisible Nation: Homeless Families in America* (Berkeley, CA, 2016)

Thomas, James, *From Tennessee Slave to St Louis Entrepreneur: The Autobiography of James Thomas* (Columbia, MO, 1984)

Thomas, Jane, *Old Days in Nashville* (Nashville, TN, 1897)

Waller, William, *Nashville, 1900 to 1910* (Nashville, TN, 1972)

—, ed., *Nashville in the 1890s* (Nashville, TN, 1970)

Wood, Nicki Pendleton, *Nashville: Yesterday and Today* (Lincolnwood, IL, 2010)

Zibart, Carl, *Yesterday's Nashville* (Miami, FL, 1976)

Films and Television

Country Music, dir. Ken Burns (2019), PBS documentary

Nashville, dir. Robert Altman (1975)

Nashville was an ABC network television series, which aired from 2012 to 2018

The Green Mile, dir. Frank Darabont (1999)

The Coal Miner's Daughter, dir. Michael Apted (1980)

W. W. and the Dixie Dance Kings, dir. John G. Avildsen (1975)

Websites

www.tennessean.com

www.nashvillescene.com

www.nashvillepost.com

http://thecontributor.org

https://nashvillepublicart.com

www.explorenashvilleart.com

https://greenwaysfornashville.org
https://tnstateparks.com

Acknowledgments

I owe a deep bow of gratitude to these Nashvillians who nurtured and encouraged me in one way or another as I wrote this book: Amy and Andres Bermudez; Melanie Branscomb; John Bridges; Charles Conte; Mike and Lee Dorman; Warren Duzak; Acadia, Andrée, and Alan LeQuire; Bill Long-Innes; Ben Mueller; Elizabeth Odle; Anne Paine; Carol Rabideau; Howard Romaine; Gayle and John Rosen; Terry Katzman-Rosenblum; and Bernie Rosenblum.

Thanks as well go to the ever-helpful staff of the Ben West Public Library, and its Metropolitan Government Archives of Nashville-Davidson County, as well as to the library's Special Collections Department, and the staff of the Tennessee State Library.

Thanks also to my eagle-eyed friend Clare Bratten for a reading of the final draft. And, once again, I'd like to invoke the names of two late, great Nashvillians named John, who showed me much patience and kindness back in the day: John Egerton and John Seigenthaler. I miss them both like the dickens.

Photo Acknowledgments

The author and publishers wish to express their thanks to the below sources of illustrative material and/or permission to reproduce it. Some locations of artworks are also given below, in the interests of brevity:

Robert Altman/Michael Ochs Archives via Getty Images: p. 120; Andrew Jackson Foundation: p. 33; AngelMcNallphotography/iStock. com: pp. 180–81; photo Terri Meyer Boake/The Skyscraper Center, CTBUH, Chicago: p. 107; Bob Fitch Photography Archive, Department of Special Collections, Stanford University Libraries: p. 111; Tanner Boriack/Unsplash: p. 10 (bottom); Paul Brennan/Pixabay: pp. 11 (top), 14, 133; Brooklyn Museum, Gift of Wallace B. Putnam from the Estate of Consuelo Kanaga (82.65.2118): p. 177; photo courtesy Selina Carrisales, Plaza Mariachi: p. 127; Cartela/Shutterstock: p. 158; Jason Coleman/ Pixabay: p. 13 (bottom); photo Dr Theron Corse: p. 34; Country Music Hall of Fame and Museum, Nashville: p. 137; from Capt. Calvin D. Cowles, ed., *Atlas to Accompany the Official Records of the Union and Confederate Armies* (Washington, DC, 1891–5): p. 69; photos Warren Duzak: pp. 33 (Tennessee State Museum, Nashville), 99, 171, 182; photo courtesy Rashed Fakhruddin, president of the Islamic Center of Nashville: p. 128; Rick Friedman/Corbis via Getty Images: p. 119; photo courtesy Grant Goggins: p. 156; photo courtesy David Gonnerman, Nashville Farmers' Market: p. 163; Drew Hays/Unsplash: p. 8; Highrises.com: p. 130; Garrett Hill/ Pixabay: p. 10 (top); Brandon Jean/Unsplash: pp. 12, 13 (top); Matthew LeJune/Unsplash: p. 11 (bottom); photo Ryan Kaldari: p. 152 (top); Robert W. Kelley/The LIFE Picture Collection/Getty Images: p. 138; Library of Congress, Prints and Photographs Division, Washington, DC: pp. 15 (Carol M. Highsmith's America), 51, 52, 55, 63, 64, 66, 68, 75, 78, 82–3, 86, 170; Metro Archives, Nashville Public Library: pp. 16, 74, 88, 89, 97, 104, 108, 112, 113, 114, 116–17, 136, 152 (bottom), 179; The Metropolitan Museum of Art, New York: p. 30; Minneapolis Institute of Art, MN: p. 37; Hari Nandakumar/Unsplash: p. 191; photos courtesy Nashville Area Chamber of Commerce: pp. 19, 20, 23, 42, 124, 129, 134, 188, 189; National Archives at College Park, MD: p. 178; National Museum of the American Indian, Smithsonian Institution, Washington, DC: p. 32; National Park

Readers are free to:
share—copy and redistribute the material in any medium or format.
adapt—remix, transform, and build upon the material for any purpose,
even commercially.

Under the following terms:
attribution—You must give appropriate credit, provide a link to
the license, and indicate if changes were made. You may do so in
any reasonable manner, but not in any way that suggests the licensor
endorses you or your use.
no derivatives—If you remix, transform, or build upon the material,
you may not distribute the modified material.
share alike—If you remix, transform, or build upon the material,
you must distribute your contributions under the same license as
the original.

Index